Twayne's Theatrical Arts Series

Warren French
EDITOR

Karel Reisz

Karel Reisz directing Vanessa Redgrave
in *Isadora* (1968)

Karel Reisz

GEORG GASTON

Appalachian State University

BOSTON

Twayne Publishers

1980

Karel Reisz

Published in 1980 by Twayne Publishers
A Division of G. K. Hall & Co.

Copyright © 1980 by G. K. Hall & Co.

Printed on permanent/durable acid-free paper and bound
in the United States of America

First Printing December 1980

Library of Congress Cataloging in Publication Data

Gaston, Georg, 1938–
Karel Reisz.

(Twayne's theatrical arts series)
Bibliography: p. 154–58
Filmography: p. 159–63
Includes index.
1. Reisz, Karel.
PN1998.A3R3843   791.43'0233'0924   80-23250
ISBN 0-8057-9277-5

Contents

About the Author

GEORG M. A. GASTON was born in Kiev, Ukrania, on October 22, 1938. He came to this country in 1950 as part of a refugee program. He received his B.A. from Texas A&M University in 1962 and his M.A. and Ph.D. from Auburn University. Between getting his M.A. in 1963 and his Ph.D. in 1974, he taught English at Texas A&I University and at North Texas State University. Presently he is an associate professor in the English Department of Appalachian State University. There he teaches a variety of courses, including one in film. He has read and written a number of papers and articles on film and literature. Because of his special training and background in the modern English novel, he has developed a continuing interest in the relation between British films and novels.

Editor's Foreword

FOR REASONS that I think are characteristic of both the subject and the author of this book, the most valuable clue to understanding the career of Karel Reisz can be found, I believe, in a parenthetical remark buried in a note at the back of the book, in which author Georg Gaston points out that Karel Reisz has continued to make television commercials throughout the years "as a means of livelihood."

There are, of course, American filmmakers like John Cassavetes and some of the experimentalists whose work is difficult to see except at the Whitney Museum who finance their more ambitious projects by less satisfying work; generally, however, they are committed to making offbeat films that have little commercial potential. Karel Reisz is quite a different kind of artist.

His six major films have all been ambitious efforts to produce serious commercial entertainment. The first of them, *Saturday Night and Sunday Morning*, based on Alan Sillitoe's highly regarded novel about British working-class life, was both a critical and public success. Another, *Morgan!*, became, to, I believe, everyone's surprise, a cultist favorite among rebellious and disillusioned young people in the 1960s. Its successor, *Isadora*, should have fared better than it did; but it was poorly promoted and distributed in the United States in the dying days of the hard-ticket "road show" and then ruthlessly savaged by indiscriminate cutting in a doomed effort to recoup some of the producers' investment.

Reisz has most recently been subjected to the supreme irony of seeing his latest film, *Who'll Stop the Rain*, become an almost instant classic on the repertoire film theater circuit without first enjoying nationwide commercial circulation, probably because of the myth, now disproved by the more determined distributors of *The Deer*

Hunter and *Apocalypse Now,* that films touching upon the United States' embarrassing involvement in Vietnam are not box office. (We should observe, however, that the same curious fate has befallen such quite different films as *Blue Collar, Paradise Alley,* and *Days of Heaven.*)

I dislike such pretentious terms as "director's director"; yet unmistakably Reisz is a senior member of a generation of filmmakers whose works demand a response that general audiences cannot provide. We cannot ignore his launching his career in film by the unusual route of a book on techniques of film editing. While most serious film artists recognize that films are primarily created at the editor's table, few in the audience are capable of recognizing the subtleties of editing techniques. Reisz is an artist ahead of his time; and the most regrettable thing is that the economics of filmmaking will probably prevent his making the contribution that he should to the art.

While it would be impossible in any series that attempts a comprehensive history of filmmaking to ignore such major creators as Alfred Hitchcock and John Ford, who have satisfied both critics and the public, it has been a particular purpose of this series—like all Twayne series—to provide studies of those artists whose works have not hitherto received the scrutiny that they should. While this book is shorter than others in the series, since Karel Reisz over two decades has been responsible for only six major and controversial films, we feel that the time has come for a careful examination of such a body of work that allows an unusual opportunity for intensive study of a significant artist.

Whatever else may be said about Reisz, he has certainly not repeated himself; his six films do offer materials for almost a textbook study of film art—an adaptation of a popular, angry working-class novel, a reinterpretation of a horror classic, a mixture of pop politics and absurd humor in a tale of marital discord and madness, a probing of the career of a revolutionary artist, a clinical study of an uncontrollable compulsive, and a speculation upon the demoralizing aftereffects of United States involvement in Vietnam.

Despite the variety of the subjects and the timeliness of most of them, an underlying unity is apparent in Reisz's work. All of his films deal with principal characters who are oppressed and frustrated by their environments. A common sensibility unites them, a sensibility that Georg Gaston identifies with the observation in his opening sentence that Reisz is, like many of his characters, "a displaced person."

Even though Reisz has had the advantage of working in England, his films reflect the same sensibility as those of his Czech compatriots. *Saturday Night and Sunday Morning* and *Morgan!* are very close in spirit and even substance to *Black Peter* and *Loves of A Blonde;* and all of Reisz's films have touched upon the same problems of individuality, madness, and bureaucratic restraints as, for example, Milos Forman's *One Flew Over the Cuckoo's Nest.* Both as a child in a Czechoslovakia terrorized by the Nazi German menace and as a young man seeing his homeland sovietized, Reisz has faced but escaped the dehumanizing effects of surrendering his individual vision to bureaucratic protocols; yet he has retained a sense not easily available to Americans of how close to the surface of everyday "business as usual" oppressive madness lurks. His films emerge, like Jerzy Kosinski's novels, from the sensibility of one who has narrowly escaped the regimenting of his personality; and we could wish that Reisz might yet have the opportunity to interpret on the screen some of Kosinski's novels.

Georg Gaston is ideally suited for the analysis of Reisz's work, which he readily identifies as "a labor of love," because, like his subject, he was also the youthful beneficiary of a refugee program that has put him into a position in which he is free to explore the significance of his own early experiences. I confess that I had never really appreciated Reisz's achievement until I looked at his films through Professor Gaston's eyes; he opened up a world that I was glad not to have shared, but that I feel I and all Americans should become acquainted with if we are ever to use our freedom to avoid the excruciating effects of our naive errors that have caught us up in matters like the Iranian embassy crisis, which involves us even as I write. I can well understand the reasons for Professor Gaston's deep attraction to Reisz, and I am pleased that we are able to add to this series a book by and about what may well be called "kindred spirits."

I hope that this book will lead to further study and appreciation of a filmmaker whose uncommon blending of style and substance have not been hitherto sufficiently appreciated, because I feel that one of our most serious American failings has been an inadequate appreciation of subtlety on the rare occasions we are offered it. If I were asked, on the basis of my own viewing of Reisz's films and my reading of Georg Gaston's book, the major virtue of his subject's work, I would say it is that it is consistently understated. To return to that revelatory note that launched this discussion, I am intrigued by Georg Gaston's statement that Reisz finds that a "highly condensed and disciplined" form like the TV commercial can be charged with suggestive meaning. In a world that thrives on overstatement, the rare quality of understatement is likely not to be "box office"; but one hopes that it will finally make its point.

W. F.

Preface

THIS BOOK BEGAN several years ago during a class discussion in a film course I was teaching. As I remember it, that was one of those times when teaching really does appear to be its own reward. When that class period was over, I was in a state of elation. I felt sure that this time, at least, I had managed to impress upon my students some valuable lessons about the art of movies.

The film which we had all seen and were then ready to discuss in class was *Saturday Night and Sunday Morning*. I had loved the movie, but I couldn't be certain that my students would feel the same way. It was, after all, so different from the kind they were used to seeing, apparently so plain yet extremely subtle and crafty. Thus when I walked into the classroom, I was fully prepared to give a lecture on the merits of the film rather than lead a discussion as I preferred to do.

I needn't have worried. The class wanted to talk. Everybody seemed to be enthusiastic about the film and curious about its director.

The amazing thing was that this enthusiasm was directed primarily at the style of the film. This is what I hoped would happen each time we met. Too often, however, the class was more interested in talking about the plot and the stars of the film which we had seen.

But here was a film which inspired their imaginations in a different way. It managed to make them see more clearly than they had before how important the way a film is told could actually be, that indeed the style of a film could be the real issue. That the style might not merely convey the story, but go so far as to contain its essential point or theme.

In the course of this class discussion, two questions naturally arose. Who was this man Reisz anyway, and what else had he done? All I could tell my students at the time was that I knew only a few common facts about him. He had written a book on the technique of film editing which was highly regarded. He had been involved in the Free Cinema movement in Britain. And he had made some other movies which had received a measure of critical praise. Beyond that I was in the dark, so little had been written expressly about him. I recall adding that it seemed a shame that Reisz had been ignored so much, and that it was time that someone did a full-length study of his work. Why not you, some class wit wanted to know. I turned him off with the blithe statement that I might think about it.

Once I actually started on the book, I knew that its heart would certainly have to deal with film style. This was, after all, what had excited my students about Reisz's work in the first place. Besides, as my investigation proceeded, what had at first been a strong feeling about Reisz had become a conviction. Here was a true master of film language and technique. If I could write a book which would illustrate this, I felt, it would have some real merit. It would benefit those readers who simply wished to know more about Reisz's work. In addition, it would benefit those who wished to discover more about how film style can work as a whole.

As far as biographical and background information were concerned, I decided to include as much as would tend to be of help in the appreciation and interpretation of Reisz's individual films. With these goals in mind, I also decided to put some emphasis on acting. This I felt I must do because Reisz's movies are almost always marked by very fine acting. If that is the case, it is not by accident. The truth seems to be that Reisz is one of those directors with the talent for eliciting the very best from a cast.

Now that the book is finished, I wonder why it is still the first on Reisz. Some possible answers come immediately to mind. He doesn't fit neatly into the pattern which the *auteur* theory calls for. He makes films slowly, and people forget quickly. He doesn't appear to have the flair or desire for self-promotion.

My intention is not, of course, to *promote* Reisz with this book. Obviously, his reputation will have to depend ultimately on his whole body of work. My role, as I see it, is mainly to call critical attention to his individual films. As it happens, I think that he has made a number of very impressive ones. And I trust that others are on the way. Meanwhile, I hope that more will now appear on the printed page about Reisz and his work. It does seem to be high time.

GEORG GASTON

Appalachian State University

Acknowledgments

IN WRITING this book I had some valuable help for which I would like to express my gratitude. I especially wish to thank Jane Stilling for helping me administer the film rental grant which I received from Appalachian State University for my project; the British Film Institute for providing me on a couple of occasions with important research information on Reisz; Warren French for his enthusiastic encouragement and very helpful suggestions; and my wife, Karen. Her love and understanding of movies were a constant source of inspiration to me. Unless otherwise credited, illustrations were provided by Movie Star News, New York City.

Chronology

1926   Karel Reisz is born in Ostrava, Czechoslovakia, on July 21.

1938   Comes to Britain as a refugee.

1945–   Attends Emmanuel College, Cambridge.
1947

1947–   Teaches at the Grammar School of Marylebone.
1949

1950   Begins to contribute criticism to *Sequence* and *Sight and Sound*.

1952   Begins to serve a three-year tenure as program director of the National Film Theatre.

1953   *The Technique of Film Editing* is published.

1956   Codirects *Momma Don't Allow* with Tony Richardson.

1957   Coproduces Lindsay Anderson's *Every Day Except Christmas* with Leon Clore.

1959   Directs *We Are The Lambeth Boys*.

1960   Directs *Saturday Night and Sunday Morning*.

1963   Produces Lindsay Anderson's *This Sporting Life*.

1964   Directs *Night Must Fall*.

1966   Directs *Morgan!*

1968   Directs *Isadora*.

1973   Directs *On the High Road*, a film made for television.

1974   Directs *The Gambler*.

1978   Directs *Who'll Stop the Rain*.

1

The Early Years

THE FIRST THING that might be noted about Karel Reisz is that, like so many of his film characters, he knows what it is to be a displaced person. He was born on July 21, 1926, in Ostrava, a small town in Czechoslovakia. There his early childhood years were spent in comfortable security. His father, Josef, could see to that as a lawyer. But when Reisz was twelve years old, he was suddenly uprooted. Because of the growing Nazi threat, it was decided that he should join a convoy of refugee children bound for England. The hope might have been otherwise, but this turned out to be a permanent kind of removal. The convoy succeeded in bringing the boy to safety. His parents, however, staying behind, were fated to die in a concentration camp.

Reisz's parents had previously sent his older brother, Paul, to a Quaker boarding school in England, the Leighton Park School in Reading. This school sponsored Reisz's place in the transport of children and then took him in as a refugee when he landed in England. And it was this school which would provide him with a basic English education as well as a home while he grew up.[1]

When he landed in his new home, it was with scarcely a word of English. His initial adjustment, though, was very quick and eager. In fact, as he now recalls, he soon wished more than anything to become as English as possible.[2] Beyond that adolescent ambition, however, he gave no clear indication of what else he might ultimately wish to be for a number of years. No doubt this was in large part due to the violent disruption caused by the outbreak of the Second World War.

Because of the war, some important decisions were thrust upon

17

At the London jazz club in Momma Don't Allow

Credit: British National Film Archive

Reisz while he was still very young. In 1944 he joined the Czech-oslovakian wing of the RAF. He was trained as a fighter pilot, but the hostilities ended before he saw any combat. The following year, with the war finally over, he was repatriated and traveled back to Czechoslovakia with his military unit. Shortly afterwards, however, he managed to get a leave of absence to go back to England. This leave was granted so that he could study at Cambridge University, where he had obtained entrance while he had still been in England. Between 1945 and 1947 he studied the natural sciences, particularly chemistry, as a member of Emmanuel College. When he was through with his schooling, however, he didn't choose to go back to Czechoslovakia. Instead, he took up a teaching position at the Grammar School of Marylebone. Here he stayed between 1947 and 1949.

It was in 1949 that he gave the first clear evidence of what his destiny would actually be. That is when he tried his hand at film criticism. Needless to say, he was very successful in this area. By the following year he was an important contributor to the Oxford University Film Society magazine, *Sequence,* finally collaborating with Lindsay Anderson on coediting its last number in 1952.[3] Also starting in 1950, but lasting until 1958, he began to contribute criticism to Britain's foremost film journal, *Sight and Sound.* And in 1953 he came forth with an important book, *The Technique of Film Editing.*

The Technique of Film Editing

This book has since become a kind of classic, as close to a definitive work on the art and practice of editing as is available. Amazingly enough, before Reisz wrote it he had yet to do any editing on his own. On the other hand, this lack of experience was precisely one of the major reasons he was selected by the sponsors of the book, the British Film Academy. As Reisz recalls, the original idea was that the Academy "wanted to find a journalist as Boswell to a lot of senior British directors and editors."[4] Reisz played this role very well, of course. But he obviously went much further. Once he began the project, he was clearly driven by a great intellectual curiosity and downright obsessive energy. Thorold Dickinson, who was close to the project as the chairman of the Academy, perhaps best recalls just how far Reisz threw himself into his work. As he remembers it, Reisz worked "over months of gruelling experiment" while he "patiently sifted the relevant technique from the personal reminiscence and . . . projected miles of film in search of the apt sequence, analysing on a hand projector the chosen sequences, noting every detail and measuring every foot."[5]

The result of all this intense work was a book which covers the subject of film editing in a most exhaustive way. It begins with a section on the history of editing theories and practices, focusing first on the silent era and some of its giants and then proceeding to the sound era. In the next section the functional side of editing is taken up. As it turns out, this is actually the heart of the book. Here examples of all types are carefully analyzed—ranging all the way from action, dialogue, and comedy sequences to newsreels and compilation films. In the third and final section, the conclusions about the art of editing which might logically follow are drawn together into a discussion of the principles of editing.

It should be emphasized that this book was meant to be primarily analytical in nature. However, because it succeeds so well in this endeavor, it becomes something more than just a practical handbook. In the end, it also serves to express in a very convincing way a theoretical attitude about editing. This is that editing is no doubt the primary creative force of filming because the fashion in which the pictures and the sounds of a movie are put together is not only inextricably linked with the content but actually drives its meaning in the most essential way.

Reisz learned a great deal from writing this book and from the experience of working with some enthusiastic film professionals who helped him with the project. As a result, he may have felt more than ever ready and eager to get into the business of making, not just writing about, movies. Before he got his chance to do so, however, he was forced to continue what amounted to his apprenticeship.

From 1952 to 1955 he served as the programming director of the National Film Theatre. Then a 16mm amateur film led him into the film division of the Ford Motor Company. There he served as the officer of commercials for a number of months between 1956 and 1957. This job was hardly inspirational, since it consisted primarily of making commercials about tractors, motors, and cars. Still, it provided Reisz with some valuable practical experience.[6] Moreover, when Ford decided to sponsor a number of documentaries on British life, he found himself in a position where he was allowed to do creative work to which he could apply some of the principles of a movement of which he was a part, the movement which came to be called "Free Cinema."

Free Cinema

This portentous title refers to a loosely organized, rather isolated movement in the history of British cinema. Generally speaking, it was a phenomenon which saw several young filmmakers brought together, both by accident and design, by certain artistic goals and a common desire to find an outlet for their work. More specifically, it consisted of a series of programs shown at the National Film Theatre in London and the creative atmosphere which these films for a time generated and expressed.

This movement didn't actually live for very long. In fact, only six programs where shown under its banner at the National Theatre—beginning in February 1956 and ending in March 1959. However, while it lasted it managed to bring together and to display a great deal of fresh and exciting talent. The core of the movement consisted of the same young men who had been leading contributors to *Sequence*. But "Free Cinema" also attracted the participation of such people as Norman McLaren, Tony Richardson, Lionel Rogosin, and Alain Tanner.[7]

Lindsay Anderson, the recognized leader of this informal movement, has since declared that "Free Cinema" was really "nothing more than a label of convenience" and that its programs were "never planned as anything other than a way of showing our work."[8] But this is surely an oversimplification. For as Anderson no doubt must have realized at the time, the label which he himself invented fit the pictures being shown under it perfectly in a number of important ways.

To begin with, "Free Cinema" helped to liberate some young filmmakers from the usual way of doing business. Which is to say, it encouraged them to make movies outside the existing framework of production, to strike out on their own. In Britain this meant, most specifically, to work outside the constraints of either the Ealing Studio tradition or the Rank factory system. That was no small matter, since these two institutions had dominated the film industry for many years. But in the mid-1950s the industry found itself in sufficiently serious trouble to encourage a rebellion from those on the outside. This is, of course, where the young members of "Free Cinema" came in. Recognizing that the time was right, they decided, in the words of Reisz, that they would "take things into our own hands and become film authors."[9]

When the works of these young "authors" began to appear in the context of "Free Cinema," they were accompanied by a series of program notes which defined the aims of the movement. These amounted to an artistic declaration of independence, rather sweeping in implication and yet ultimately expressing the absolute necessity of three forms of freedom. First, these filmmakers insisted on the importance of being allowed to use nonfiction films as a means of expressing their deepest personal feelings and beliefs. In addition, they argued vigorously for the right of the director to fully control his movie. Finally, they insisted that they be left free to use techniques in their pictures which were poetic. Poetic in the sense, as Anderson himself put it, "of larger implications than the surface realities may suggest," with the "most important challenge" being "to get beyond pure naturalism into poetry."[10]

In retrospect, it's clear that the "Free Cinema" movement was rewarding to Reisz in two essential ways. On one hand, it helped him to gain a theoretical foundation. The tenets of artistic freedom which were generally espoused by the movement very nearly describe the primary obsessions of Reisz during the course of the career which followed. This is especially clear when the question of style enters in. It is always "poetic" in the sense that Anderson uses the word. On the other hand, the movement provided him with a basic training, a chance to actually put theory into practice.

Momma Don't Allow

Reisz's first full, direct work with "Free Cinema" was on the picture *Momma Don't Allow*. He was limited to being its codirector. Luckily, though, the other codirector was Tony Richardson. Working closely together, and obviously learning from the experience and from each other as they went along, they managed to create a film which was one of the highlights of the very first "Free Cinema" program.

Momma Don't Allow deals with a London jazz club and its enthusiasts during what appears to be a typical evening for them.
There is the barest suggestion of a story line. The film simply begins
by following three young people as they meet their partners and
some "Teddy Boys" to go to a club for music and dancing. At the
club they are observed responding in a variety of ways to the music
and to each other. Now and then a humorous or romantic incident
is spotlighted. Basically, however, the scene is depicted in a highly
objective, even remote way.

The idea behind this detached strategy seemed to be, in the
words of Lewis Jacobs, to let the camera act as a "casual spectator,
focusing upon the passing moment and letting it speak for itself."[11]
There are times, unfortunately, when *Momma Don't Allow* speaks
so quietly that the point may be lost on the casual spectator. At
other times the camera style is so languid that the point becomes
overextended and thus may be lost in another manner. On the
whole, however, the style is well chosen.

In what is still the best single article on "Free Cinema," Gavin
Lambert wrote the following about *Momma Don't Allow:* "The film
celebrates a piece of urban folklore in the making. The movements
created by the young dancers are often surprisingly complex and
beautiful; evolving out of the music, of the mood as it comes and
goes, they also suggest a curious abstraction from life. Costume
plays a minor part . . . and at times the couples seem wholly remote
from each other, each dancer preoccupied with his own movements,
creating his own vacuum, occasionally, as if by chance, coming
together for a moment with his partner; at other times an instinctive
rapport apparently exists between a couple, and the excitement,
the rhythmic responses, are shared."[12] Lambert doesn't himself
claim as much, but it seems obvious that these moments of escape,
abstraction, and identification come through as effectively as they
do largely because of the camera strategy which was chosen. The
film has a consciously spontaneous yet passive style. And because
of this, the viewer is allowed to discover what is natural and vital
to the young jazz enthusiasts mainly on his own.

As Lambert went on to say, however, despite "all its attractive
skill, its sympathetic and unforced presentation of people . . . the
film is not quite a personal statement. It wants to do more than
record, but when it sets out to interpret . . . it seems hampered
by a note of reservation, it becomes almost commonplace."[13] This

sort of confusion or indecisiveness had, no doubt, at least two good explanations. First, it revealed the fact that the two young codirectors still had quite a bit to learn about their craft. Second, it showed that, when making a movie, it's better to have just one instead of two strong minds in charge.

Reisz was, of course, eager to strike out on his own. It would be about three more years before he got his chance. Then, with the aid of the British Film Institute's Experimental Fund as well as that of the Ford Motor Company, he managed to make what is now considered by many people to be the finest product of the "Free Cinema" movement—*We Are the Lambeth Boys*.

We Are the Lambeth Boys

We Are the Lambeth Boys deals with a London youth club and some of its members at work and at play. A modest enough project, it seems, but it leaves an extraordinary impression. That is because, when the film ends, one senses that it has been about something timeless, the essence of youth.

There is nothing exceptional about the early part of the film, as a matter of fact. It begins with a written message quietly praising the advantages of the club. Then a commentator briefly adds to the praise, introduces us to some of the members, and begins to serve the role of making the progression of the film as smooth and clear as possible.

The commentator also has the traditional function of spokesman for the beliefs of the filmmakers; and at those points the film is at its weakest. At least, this seems obvious today. The problem is that some of the mildly sentimental beliefs espoused by the commentator seem now to be naive or simply mistaken. The thoughts about the importance of work, however dull and unrewarding it might be, sound impertinent. The rather paternal attitude taken toward the boisterous energy of the young appears curiously dated to anyone who has lived through the 1960s. These and other such comments no doubt had the best intentions behind them. Still, they now sound strangely lifeless if not obsolete.

The film as a whole, however, is vivid—in a schizoid way. This is due to a tension existing between the mildly liberal politics of the filmmakers and the radical poetic urge of Reisz. To put it another

We Are the Lambeth Boys—socializing at a fish and chips place after an evening at the club

[Credit: British National Film Archive]

way, on the practical level, the film sets out to teach the public a social lesson; on the artistic level, it hopes to make the public *imagine* sympathetically what it means to be young under certain conditions. The film starts out on the first level, and it ends on the second. It is as if Reisz, growing in assurance as the film progresses, gives more and more rein to his imagination. The result is that, by the time he finishes the documentary, Reisz has learned to express what is vital about his subject through a refined, complex technique.

Film Style and Key Scenes

This technique, which allows Reisz to be both objective as well as analytical at the same time, can be seen most clearly at work in some key scenes. One is where the young members meet in one of the rooms of the club to debate the death penalty.

First, the transition between this scene and the previous one is significant. In the previous scene some of the young people are quietly and happily drawing and painting. The camera looks over their shoulders now and again, and it discovers what appear to be their personal fantasies or obsessions. The last picture we see is of a hold-up. As the camera focuses on it, there is a voice-over, vaguely heard at first, and then, with a cut, it loudly proclaims a personal bias about capital punishment.

All the young people seem to have passionate feelings on this subject, and they all announce them loudly. As they do, the camera moves without plan, like the discussion, from face to face, most of the time focusing on the speaker of the moment, but sometimes dwelling on a particularly revealing facial reaction. It acts like an interested but neutral observer. The fact that it is placed at an eye-level medium distance serves to add to this impression.

Suddenly the camera cuts up and back, as if to imply that it is time to analyze the drift of the discussion, to put it in perspective. Then the eye-level, medium distancing is quickly reestablished. Only now, while the camera goes from one excitable face to another, a sassy, almost teasing saxophone starts to come in.

At this point the commentator intrudes. This is unfortunate because without any editorial words Reisz has already expressed the wonderful energy, idealism, and confusion of these young people. It is redundant for the commentator to say that it's good to have strong feelings but that knowledge is also needed. One is led to suspect that Reisz, having once been a teacher, could not resist repeating the main point of a lesson.

Fortunately, the commentator is characteristically brief, and the scene has a splendid ending. After the commentary is over, the music picks up in tempo and the camera cuts in a deliberate rhythm from face to face. Each face is all smiles and laughter now, however. Thus the final impression, supported by the technique throughout this scene, is of the volatile, spontaneous, and generous nature of youth.

Another key scene takes us to the school where two of the members of the club still go. This scene is even more effective than the one dealing with the death penalty discussion. Partly this is due to the fact that the commentator, with the exception of a few words about the importance of work, is used with more tact. More important, in this scene Reisz has learned to use what might be called antithetical montage with great effect.

The scene begins after a long fade-out, fade-in transition, thus emphasizing the difference between the excitement of the previous night at the club and the dreariness of the morning. It is now time to put in a day at work or at school. First we go to school, where the scene is touching in a depressing way. The school day begins with a hymn. As the assembly of boys starts to sing, we are touched by the pensive beauty of the scene. At this point the camera is placed so that the point of view seems to be that of one of the teachers on the dais. Then the camera cuts closer to pick out the boy named Bryan. He has a beautiful, sad tenor voice, which now is raised and purposely distinguished from the other voices.

After this, as we continue to hear his quite angelic singing, the scene shifts to some of the other members of the club at work. They all appear to have dull, routine, more or less dead-end jobs.

The camera shows us five of the young people at work, and then it shifts back to the pensive face of Bryan as the hymn comes to a close. The inevitable impression left is sadly ironic. The hymn, and the boy's imagination, may be full of the finest sentiments. But the future for this youth and those around him, largely because of the existence of the British class system, is no doubt rather dismal.

This point is stressed forcefully as the scene continues. After the hymn ends, the assembly of boys prays. Then there is a dissolve back to the same five young people still at work. This time, though, the camera dwells more on two particular workers. One is a girl, Beryl, who works on an assembly line. It is an extremely monotonous, dreary job. And Beryl's face expresses her boredom with it very clearly. The other is a boy, Bobby, who works at the post office. His face, too, is a picture of boredom. In the future his job might get a bit more interesting, since in time he may be allowed to drive a service vehicle. Until then, however, he is trapped inside doing work which isn't fundamentally different from Beryl's. This point is emphasized by a transitional image which links the two jobs. In the case of Beryl, the camera focuses for some time on circular containers moving down the assembly line. In the case of Bobby, it focuses on the round button of the stapler which the boy uses as he goes through stacks of forms.

The way Reisz presents Bobby's stapling job, which comes at the end of this important scene, is most revealing. The camera usually looks down on the stapler as the boy slams his hand down on it again and again. We hear the sound of the stapler, until suddenly there is the use of subjective sound. To suggest Bobby's drifting mind, we hear not the stapler but a conversation which he perhaps has recently overheard or taken part in. We are not sure, only that whatever its original source it is now once more taking place in his mind. Then, in a striking switch, the sound of the stapler is heard again, except that this time it loudly reverberates, like a gun shot. This is followed by a contrasting short period of silence, during which the camera shows us Bobby's bored face once again. Nothing else is needed. This silent image summarizes perfectly the intent of this key scene—that such dreary, monotonous work will deaden the spirit.

An analysis of the other major scenes in the film would show some of the same dynamics at play as those found in the two key scenes just discussed. But it is in the final scene that Reisz shows that he has learned to employ the most difficult aspect of a poetic style—purposeful ambiguity. The final scene begins when a particularly lively Saturday-night dance at the club ends. The camera follows the young people out to the streets, where they linger together as long as they can before it is time to break up to go home. When they finally are pictured going home in twos and threes, the scene becomes naturally dark because of the weak street lighting. When the last youth is seen heading toward his home, however, he seems to be actually overcome by a deep blackness. It is an eerie moment, and the start of what appears to be Reisz's final, pessimistic comment on the subject of this documentary.

Two brief shots follow, and the darkness (of the young people's future?) is emphasized again. After the last youth disappears into the dark void, the camera cuts to a long shot. Now we can see the many lighted windows of the flats, but they look forlorn, ghostly. The camera then pans to the right, as if it were searching for something, and then a train whistle is heard, followed by a silence. As the camera holds still, we begin to distinguish a factory building, tall cranes, and a skeleton of a new building. Or we appear to see these things.

Why end this way? The answer seems to have everything to do with mood. The mood, contrasting so starkly with the buoyancy of much of the film, is profoundly mournful. The dark shapes of the last shot, belonging to the bleak working-class world which faces the youth, grow in the imagination like phantoms. The film begins with the exuberance of youth, but it appears to end with the despair of lost illusions.

A Limited Response

In his article on *We Are the Lambeth Boys,* in the form of an open letter to Reisz, Richard Hoggart praised the documentary for its many fine points; but he went on to suggest that Reisz should try in the future to make film essays which would focus more clearly on the inner life of people.[14] Reisz's answer, in retrospect, was that he also wished that he could have gone further in the "Free Cinema" genre, but that financial conditions made it impossible. In his own words, he felt that the makers of such films "were only at the very beginning . . . . *But there simply is no money or audience for this kind of movie in the English Cinema.* . . . I spent two years as the full-time film officer at the Ford Motor Company, doing their advertising on condition they gave me money for . . . two pictures, and you simply can't spend your life like that for long periods. Besides, we never found an audience for the pictures. (The booking fee for *We Are the Lambeth Boys,* in circuit houses where it played as a second feature, was £ 5!)."[15]

Inevitably, then, *We Are the Lambeth Boys* was Reisz's last such film. This was unfortunate, of course, for that small part of the public which did have an interest in seeing more such films. And it was unfortunate for Reisz himself, since he now recalls how making it allowed "a sense of freedom, of improvisation, of direct response to life which is very precious and very hard to find an equivalent for with a feature film crew and budget."[16] Nevertheless, Reisz was eager to try his hand at a feature film. His chance soon came, in fact the following year, and the result was a splendid success.

2

Saturday Night and Sunday Morning

THERE ARE certain novels which are destined, it seems, to be turned into movies. Such a novel was Alan Sillitoe's *Saturday Night and Sunday Morning*. Its central character, Arthur Seaton, is a hard-working, hard-drinking young rogue who seizes our attention because of his aggressive, vital spirit. He lives in a bleak factory town which has defeated the joy of living in most of its people. But Arthur has such an energetic and rebellious nature that he lives more intensely than anyone around him. Meanwhile, he also gets into continuous trouble, usually in the form of sex or violence. His most dramatic problems result from an affair with a married woman, Brenda. He impregnates her, and this leads to recrimination, guilt, and even violence. A more subtle form of trouble results from his attraction to Doreen, a young woman who has marriage on her mind. She may be physically very alluring; but her ultimate dreams of safe conformity are bound to threaten Arthur's angry independence.

Obviously, such a story is related in theme and subject matter to *Look Back in Anger*, originally a play about another angry young man. This play, written by John Osborne, was turned into one of the most important movies of the 1950s by Tony Richardson. Because of this great success, Richardson was naturally asked to be the director of the film version of *Saturday Night*, too. However, when he chose instead to be the producer, the job of director fell to Reisz. Now, finally, Reisz had the chance to make the sort of movie he had had in mind for a period of time, a kind of refinement of *We Are the Lambeth Boys*.

31

Albert Finney in a pensive mood in Saturday Night and Sunday Morning

In *Saturday Night*, as Reisz later said, he could at last concentrate on a central character who "is,.if you like, one of the Lambeth Boys. An attempt is made to make a movie about the sentimental and social education of *one specific* boy: thus the 'inner' things which the *Lambeth Boys* type of picture simply cannot apprehend . . . was attempted in *Saturday Night and Sunday Morning*. To put it more simply, and risking pretentiousness, the first work attempted a picture of a world, the second a portrait."[1] There is no doubt that the film succeeds in presenting such a portrait. However, even though Reisz doesn't here make the claim, it also tries and manages to capture Arthur's general, outward milieu in great detail. As a result, *Saturday Night* turns out to be compelling in the same way as the finest products of Italian neorealism. Like those films, *Saturday Night* has that absorbing combination of subjective as well as social analysis of an individual and his contemporary world.

Preparations

Much of the strength of the film depends on its wonderful screenplay. Because Reisz worked closely with Sillitoe on the script, it is not easy to draw a clear line between their particular contributions to it. It seems safe to say, however, that most of the credit for the vivid dialogue must go to Sillitoe. As for the final form of the movie's story, it appears that Reisz played the more important role. As a result, a novel consisting of loosely connected episodes was transformed into a film which has a wholly organic shape and a definite thematic focus.

Unlike the novel, the film has neither any excrescences in the plot nor any uncontrolled biases. The final script has discarded, for example, a halfwit girl and a Negro soldier who appear in the novel. What is retained is everything which might fit perfectly into a condensed, unified picture of Arthur Seaton and his world. As a consequence, the film has something of the paradoxical nature of classical art. It is intricate yet simple, dispassionate yet involved. It also has a complex, formal style. And it is this style which is ultimately the most expressive aspect of the film.

Reisz worked hard on arriving at a style which would be appropriate for the subject matter. That is something he, of course, struggles to accomplish in all of his films. As it turned out, in *Saturday Night* he managed to join style and content as well as he ever did.

This was partly due to the good fortune of having a creative working relationship with people as talented as Sillitoe. However, it resulted even more from his own penchant for exhaustive, analytical planning. In his own words, Reisz works in "a painstaking, stamp-collector's way. . . . I like to have it all at my fingertips before I start. It is a form of fear, I suppose."[2] This sort of anxiety impels Reisz to make films which invariably have thoroughness of detail. At the same time, this compulsion also usually leads to analytical depth. It is when these two strands of realism and analysis come together perfectly that Reisz's style is clearly most effective. At such time, Reisz is capable of "tunnelling more deeply than most into a layer of human life at a particular time and place."[3] Certainly this happened in *Saturday Night*.

Reisz believes that "the only way to get to know a place is to work there."[4] Therefore, in preparation for the making of *Saturday Night* he took a small crew to Nottingham and its surrounding area to get fully acquainted with that highly industrial region which is the setting for Sillitoe's story. He even went so far as to shoot a dry run for the film in the form of a documentary about a welfare center for miners. Sillitoe, who wrote the commentary, admits that the result was "not a very good film."[5] Nevertheless, the experience was invaluable in at least two ways. For one thing, it made it much easier for Reisz to keep the shooting of *Saturday Night* to a very tight schedule. The budget allowed for only six weeks of shooting, including only one night for an enormous fair scene.[6] Moreover, because making the dry-run documentary allowed him to gain a true feeling for the region and its way of life, Reisz learned to avoid something that he feared as he prepared to make *Saturday Night*—the appearance or suspicion that the film was "going slumming."[7] This obsession with the authenticity of the setting was a natural outgrowth of his previous experience with "Free Cinema." As a matter of fact, it remains one of the most significant characteristics to be found in his work to this day. That is, whenever the economics of filmmaking allow Reisz to support this stylistic habit.

Film Style

The first thing one notices about the style of *Saturday Night* is its documentary look. There exists an initial impression that it means to shun a conscious style. It's as if the film were saying, "Here is the way it is. The camera is only there to record what goes on before it." Thus Boleslaw Sulik, the critic, is right to note that what one is bound to remember most about *Saturday Night* is not a "cinematic style" but the incisive character study of Arthur and the careful observation of the rich human texture surrounding him.[8] Yet a careful analysis of the film will show that this rich illusion of reality was the result of an exceedingly careful strategy and that the classic style of the film is not as totally self-effacing and detached as so many critics believe.

The use of the camera is a revealing case in point. Several critics have commented on the neutral character of Freddie Francis's camera in this film. Actually, though in a quite subtle way, the camera is thoroughly involved in what it is recording. It is generally placed at such a moderate distance as to allow for objective yet intimate observation at the same time. As a result, when an extremity is used, the effect is startling. In the close-ups, for example (and there are more close-ups than the critics as a whole seem to remember), we are suddenly forced to identify with the characters who at that time are usually undergoing a crisis. In the long shots of the grimy city, we are pulled back to an overview of the environment which seems to have a deterministic effect on the characters. This tension between moderate and extreme distancing is employed throughout the film in a rhythmic way, until distancing becomes one of Reisz's most expressive means of commenting on the situation before us.

As for camera angles, the same dynamics are employed. Most of the film is shot at eye level. When there is an occasional high angle shot, the effect is immediately revealing. Thus when the camera looks down on workers streaming out of a factory, for example, we recognize at once how small and impoverished their lives are. Or when there is a shot down on rows and rows of similar houses crowded on top of each other, we see clearly how depressingly conforming life can be in an industrial city. As for low angle shots, the most revealing one shows Arthur early in the story. In a stupor after winning a drinking match, he is seen from the bottom of a staircase in a pub, looking down with something of a smirk. The shot has an ironic effect, showing Arthur as he then sees himself— unvanquished again. Then, suddenly, he falls down the stairs, and as the camera next looks down on him lying on the floor with a foolish smile on his face, we have in a way been told through the use of angles what Arthur's fate is bound to be.

Albert Finney as Arthur Seaton, tense and relaxed with his lady friends: (top) with Shirley Anne Field as Doreen and (bottom) with Rachel Roberts as Brenda.

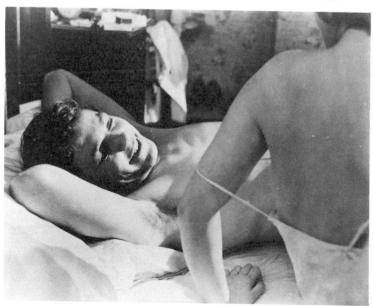

That Arthur's fate is bound up with his surroundings is often expressed through some wonderful deep focus photography. Through this means, the dramatic action which takes place close to the camera is time and again thrown into significant relief. Hence it is interesting on one level to note that the film is a kind of study of manners, picking up here and there the surface life of the people who surround the principal characters. But on a deeper level, literally, the camera eye also picks out much which has a symbolic function.

Metaphors and Images

The camera picks out, for example, a number of images which suggest the entrapment of various characters—fences, a bricked-up window, narrow passageways. It also focuses on various wasteland images. Thus garbage cans seem to be ubiquitous. And the natural landscape could make one think of Eliot's famous poem, so dominant is the bleak impression it leaves. This feeling is particularly strong when Arthur and his friend Bert fish on a canal. Then, as the two young men fish and talk about their hopes and disillusions, the power poles, the leafless scrubs, and a battered little tree create a feeling of pervading impotence.

The fishing metaphor, incidentally, appears to be somewhat forced. When the two friends first go fishing soon after Arthur meets Doreen, the connection between fishing and "getting caught" is quite transparent. Bert makes the comment that Doreen "looks different. First kiss and she'll expect an engagement ring." Arthur responds that he takes "a tip from the fishes—never bite unless the bait's good. I won't get married until I'm good and ready." Yet a short time later he says: "Take a few tips from the fishes. They all get caught in the end, though, don't they? Can't keep their chops off the bait. Wasn't a bad-looking girl though, was she? Sharp an' all." Arthur has clearly taken the bait. In a subsequent shot, Arthur pulls a sad little fish out of the canal and, sure enough, in the next scene, the final one, he and Doreen are talking about their future together.

The fishing imagery is the only kind, however, which appears to be too self-conscious. Much more subtle and thus effective is the mirror imagery. Arthur, certainly not lacking in vanity, is seen looking into a mirror three times. The first time he is putting the finishing touches on himself as he prepares for a night out with Brenda. Actually, he is then only seen in profile looking at himself. In a literal sense, he is looking off the screen into the void. The second time he is embracing Brenda and looking at himself in action, but with a strange expression, as if he were wondering what that reflection meant. The third time is after he is beaten up because of his affair with Brenda by two swaddies, one of whom is the brother of her husband. And this time he seems to be full of self-realization. Just before he looks into the mirror, he thinks to himself: "They'd beat me right enough. Still, I'd had me bit of fun. It ain't the first time I've been in a losing fight. Won't be the last either, I don't suppose. How long have I been lying here though? A week? Can't think. . . . Mum called me barmy when I told her I fell off a gas works for a bet. But I'm not barmy. I'm a six foot prop that wants a pint of beer, that's what." Then, looking into the mirror, he adds: "But if any knowing bastard tells them that's me, I'll tell 'em I'm a dynamite dealer, waiting to blow the factory to Kingdom Come. I'm me and nobody else. Whatever people say I am, that's what I'm not. Because they don't know a bloody thing about me. God knows what I am." The words of this interior monologue obviously reveal a great deal about the confused, violently conflicting nature of Arthur. But it is the mirror which functions to effectively emphasize the ironic truth about him. When Arthur looks into the mirror, he can't understand himself *because* it reflects his own image.

Another revealing image in this film is the circle, or circus, as the British might prefer. There are many graffiti signs, titles, and posters which the camera eye picks up. One of the most significant, and ironic, posters advertises a movie and reads "Life Is a Circus." It is on a wall outside Aunt Ada's house, where Arthur goes to try to get her to help with an abortion for Brenda. It is a rare bright Sunday, and while Arthur is inside talking to his aunt, Brenda waits outside with a church behind her where services are being held.

All this contrasts vividly with the fair scene later in the film. Arthur has taken Doreen there in response to her complaint that he seems to be ashamed of her because he doesn't take her any place where it's light and filled with people. The fair scene begins with our seeing Arthur and Doreen and Bert and his date Betty swinging and swooping around and around on one of the thrill rides. Reisz then cuts to Brenda, who is there with her family and the swaddies. Then, in a series of cross-cuts, the tension mounts as he cuts back and forth between Arthur and his group now riding around and around in dodgem cars and Arthur's "problems" represented by Brenda and the swaddies. When Arthur and Brenda finally notice each other, it is across the circular "roll a penny" stall. When they are forced to hide from the suspicious swaddies, they jump into a car on the roundabout. And then, in the one scene where the style does not give the appearance of being purposely subdued, they whirl about violently. Significantly, as they do, Reisz elects to use a subjective camera technique. This is appropriate, for visually, as the speed of the roundabout increases, the camera eye records an unsteady blur. It is as if Arthur's way of life were being reflected on the screen.

Some of the posters and titles which are briefly seen, by the way, show one side of Reisz which isn't often recognized. He is certainly a serious filmmaker, but he appears to be fond of playing sly little jokes when there is an opportunity. Therefore, as Arthur and Doreen leave the movie theater after their first date, it is not entirely coincidental that they walk past a poster for the romantic comedy *Pillow Talk*. Nor is it mere chance that in a scene where Brenda is getting ready to meet Arthur on a tryst the cuckolded husband is sitting in an armchair reading, yes, a *Daily Mirror* with the large headlines screaming "He Was Once a *Bride*" and "Be Proud of These Men." Needless to say, these little ironic jokes flash past us, or they might be distracting.

Use of Sound

Irony is obviously a favorite device of Reisz's, for he uses it again and again in this film as well as in others to indicate his true attitude toward his subject matter. But he realizes that, to be truly effective, irony must have a light, indirect quality. This is why his most effective use of irony in *Saturday Night* lies in the realm of sound.

In the scene where Arthur is having the drinking bout, for example, an apparently inane number by a sad pub trio comments on the action. While Arthur pours down the pints, evidently because he wishes to impress Brenda in particular, the singer of the group delivers a rather absurd love song. He begins with these lines: "What do you want if you don't want money?/ What do you want if you don't want gold?/ Tell me what you want and I'll give it to you honey./ Wish you was my love, baby." Then he makes a pointing gesture, and it seems that it is directed toward Arthur. That would be ironically appropriate, of course, because these lines suggest Arthur's line with Brenda, and they even imply that what Arthur is actually giving Brenda is not real love, but the last thing she wants just now, a child. As the scene in the pub continues, these absurd lines of the song are repeated with slight variations. And then we hear another line clearly. "Oh boy . . . You're making a fool of me," it goes, and it sounds both like a warning to Brenda and a comment on the character of Arthur.

To comment both on the characters and the environment in which they struggle, Reisz employs an intricate network of sound effects. These sounds are perfectly natural, to begin with, but they accrue additional significance because they ultimately make cross-references to other sounds which are similar. Through this means life at home and at work are constantly compared. At times this connection is emphasized through the use of overlapping sound between two scenes taking place in the two worlds. For example, at one point Arthur slams down a garbage-can lid and this sound echoes as the picture cuts immediately to the roaring plant. At other times, sounds are placed farther apart, so that one only gradually begins to suspect a connection between them. One of the more cunning such examples is the ironic similarity between the sounds of the plant's whistle and that of the ubiquitous teapots.

There are other such isolated examples, but Reisz's use of sound is actually most impressive in two scenes where we hear a sort of symphonic cacophony. The movie begins by picturing Arthur at work, and before we hear him speak for the first time we hear the great noise of the machinery. The whining, roaring, squealing, and pounding are turned up to a painful point. It seems enough to split the brain. Significantly enough, in the rest of the film some of these same sounds seem to recur, both at home and on the streets, though at a lower pitch. But in the fair scene, similar sounds turn up, and are turned up, once more.

The fair scene is, of course, a kind of fatal episode for Arthur (and, to a large extent, for Brenda). After this experience, Arthur cools off his feverish way of life and becomes a somewhat quieter person. To make this point indirectly, Reisz's microphone picks up the various exciting sounds which are natural to a fair, but which also echo the sounds of Arthur's life up to this point. Appropriately enough, this symphonic noise becomes most complex, and hence most expressive, just at that point when Arthur and Brenda whirl around on the roundabout. As it happens, this is Arthur's last whirl with Brenda, and perhaps his last impression of life as a kind of violent fair.

It is totally fitting, consequently, that the two important episodes in this film which are dominated by silence occur after the fair sequence. The first is when Arthur is ambushed by the swaddies after his last ride with Brenda. They beat him severely, and when he is pictured lying face down at the end of the scene, we have to believe that his old way of life is indeed over. He may still have some fight left in him, but he is not the same person we saw the other time when he was lying down. Then he smiled up stupidly after falling down the pub's stairs. Now, in a manner of speaking, he had had some sense knocked into him.

Strangely enough, though, it seems a shame. This ambivalent feeling toward Arthur is created through a brilliant choice of technique on the part of Reisz. First, the camera pulls back from the fight itself, as if to deglamorize it and to show a certain tact. Because the fight is shown in long shot, it appears more pitiful than brutal, more a symptom of the way of life of the entire place than just of Arthur. As the men struggle furiously, they slip and fall, land some blows, but then trip and fall over each other and into the debris and the omnipresent waste cans. Two frightened people come to look through their window, but draw back. A dog barks in the deep darkness. Otherwise there is hardly any sound. The swinging fists of the swaddies do their job on Arthur once they stand him up against a brick wall, but one can't hear the blows land. In a way the fight is like an absurd, eerie struggle between ghosts. And the lack of sound is in large part responsible for this spectral impression.

After the swaddies leave, the camera moves up to reveal the battered face of Arthur. He staggers up to a water faucet, and the camera staggers with him ever so slightly. Meanwhile the music from the nearby fair begins to come in very softly, like a reminder of his past. Then, after Arthur falls down, Reisz punctuates this critical scene by using the first fade-out.

The other significant episode which takes place in nearly total silence occurs soon after the beating. This is where Arthur goes to Doreen's house for their first date since his recovery from the injuries he had sustained. Now he appears less cocky, more nervous, and surprisingly tender. After the lovers are finally left alone by Doreen's mother, they have a love scene. It is rather short, but the kiss they have seems endless. This is because of the absence of sound, which here implies that there is something final about this kiss. That, at any rate, is the instant impression which is left. We are not allowed to dwell too long on individual stylistic devices in this film, for its subtle pacing pulls one along as if he were dreaming the story.

Editing and Pacing

This dream effect is largely due to Reisz's pacing and editing, which in *Saturday Night* are really nothing short of marvelous. If this is so, it should not, of course, surprise anyone who is familiar with Reisz's book on film editing.

In his book Reisz continuously stresses the importance of the smoothness of progression. This is a conservative philosophy of editing, and one from which Reisz eventually moves away to a considerable extent. However, in *Saturday Night* the traditions of classical cutting worked perfectly for him. That's due in large part to the nature of the story. Basically, it is episodic, leading in a cause-and-effect way from confusion to a kind of resolution. By linking the various episodes closely together into a logical chain of fate, Reisz mesmerizes us into accepting the course of the story without question.

The fact that each scene seems to flow quite naturally into the next is due to the use of rather conventional forms of transitions. The use of overlapping sound to link various scenes is one form of transition which has already been mentioned. In addition, there is the use of dissolves both to link scenes and to suggest a change of time and place. When a contrast between two scenes needs to be stressed, the cut is used. When one phase of Arthur's life ends and another is about to begin, the fade is used. Twice Reisz uses wipes, but he knows full well that they can seem to be worn-out, self-conscious devices. Thus, characteristically, he uses them to make ironic visual comments about Arthur's adolescent actions—after the drinking bout scene and to begin the scene in which Arthur shoots an old gossip with an air gun.

Within the scenes, the action flows along just as smoothly, again due in large part to Reisz's employment of rather standard cutting procedures. He employs the cutting to continuity technique almost invariably, unless the occasion calls for cross-cutting to create suspense or to suggest separation or division. The most dramatic use of Reisz's cross-cutting has already been mentioned—where the focus shifts from Arthur's group to Brenda's at the fair. Another clear example of this technique is where Arthur is having a pleasant breakfast at Brenda's while her husband is on his way home. In both cases Reisz illustrates that he has a sure instinct for shifting the focus to and fro to create a fine sense of drama.

Structure

A special feeling of drama also arises from the movie's structure. It has already been noted that *Saturday Night* has a flowing, episodic quality. Consequently, it may at first appear to be inconsistent to talk about a definite structure. Nevertheless, a careful analysis of the story's action does indicate that the episodes are so arranged as not only to flow together smoothly but also to fall into strict, revealing parts.

There are at least two ways of looking at the arrangement of these parts. First, the structure of the film might be called symphonic. There is a prologue, a kind of overture, which begins the film. Arthur's interior monologue, or soliloquy, at the beginning of the film and the various shots of his environment shown both while he talks and while the credits unroll introduce the themes which are subsequently developed. These thematic strands, weaving in and out of a work which seems to have five definite sections or movements, come together to form an unavoidable conclusion and climax.

Another way of looking at the structure of the film is theatric. Like certain classical plays, it has a six-part structure. It begins, of course, with a prologue which introduces the subject matter. Then it breaks into five acts, each consisting of five scenes. These acts are so arranged that there is clearly a rising action, a denouement, and a resolution. One has only to pick out the fifth scene in each "act" of the film to see that this scheme really does exist. Thus scene 5 shows Arthur meeting Doreen and setting up a date. In scene 10 the date takes place. Arthur is thus far successful in juggling his two affairs. However, in scene 15 Arthur is at Aunt Ada's seeking an abortion for Brenda. Scene 20 is the critical scene at the fair. And scene 25, of course, can consequently be seen as the predictable result.

The Meaning of the Ending

Perhaps in part because the film's structure was ignored or left undiscovered the full meaning of the ending has often been misinterpreted. Pauline Kael, for example, refers to the sweet and happy ending of the film.[9] To be sure, this scene begins with the appearance of hope, but it ends with surrender. As the camera first focuses on a couple walking together in the distance against a backdrop of a housing estate flooded with light, we hear Arthur and Doreen talking about the peace they feel. Then, however, the camera surprises us. It pans to the left to show us Arthur and Doreen settled on the grass. The point of this is to immediately draw a depressing analogy. Arthur and Doreen, so vividly different from others in the rest of the film, must, it seems, become just another young couple who will be forced into conformity. That Arthur instinctively fears such a prospect is shown by his suddenly throwing a rock at one of the houses. It is really a futile gesture, only he doesn't quite realize it yet. Doreen asks him why he threw the rock since he might have hit the house destined for them. He says that he doesn't know, that he just felt like it, and that this won't be the last thing he'll throw. The pathos of Arthur's belligerence is ironically punctuated as he and Doreen then get up, join hands, and walk, like the first couple of this scene, toward the immense conformity of the housing estate.

Amazingly, Alan Sillitoe is another person who misinterprets the ending. To him, Arthur's final actions represent "only a temporary lapse from militancy which would revive when things got economically tougher."[10] In light of the overall form of the film, this is as unsatisfactory an interpretation of the conclusion as is Kael's. Evidently Sillitoe is confusing the somewhat autobiographical hero of his novel with the way Arthur finally appears in the film.

Not surprisingly, the most satisfactory explanation of the ending comes from Reisz himself. As he saw it, in "a metaphorical way Arthur embodied what was happening in England: he was a sad person, terribly limited in his sensibilities, narrow in his ambitions and a bloody fool into the bargain. . . . The stone-throwing is a symptom of his impotence, a self-conscious bit, telling the audience over the character's shoulder what I think of him. I wanted to continually contrast the extent to which he is an aggressor with the extent to which he is a victim of this world. I wanted the end to have this feeling of frustration. . . . "[11]

Saturday Night has sometimes been misinterpreted in another way because of a failure to distinguish between Arthur and the filmmaker. The two are in certain ways worlds apart. As Reisz himself has said, Arthur was "by no means a standard-bearer for any ideas of mine. I never work with spokesmen. All my education, my teaching experience warned me of treating people as representatives of their world, rather than giving them the dignity of individuals; and I certainly disagree strongly with the idea that Arthur Seaton embodied my values, my outlook. . . . "[12] The truth of this statement becomes quite apparent when the point-of-view of the film is considered. There are some critics who believe that the whole story is told from Arthur's point of view, but actually, as Reisz has suggested in the previous paragraph, the perspective is always double. That is, we always have a tension between the way Arthur sees things and the way Reisz does. Only, as has been already noted, Reisz's point of view is expressed indirectly, through the dynamics of style.

The Film's Reception and Acting

It is hard to believe it today, but for a while after *Saturday Night* came out it was in danger of becoming a total financial disaster. At first it had problems with the British censorship system existing at that time. Next, the British bookers were extremely reluctant to show it at all. Once it was shown, however, the film caught on by word of mouth in Britain. [13] Needless to say, what this viewing public had to say about the film had very little, if anything, to do with film style. Mass audiences are, unfortunately, quite ignorant of such things. Still, as they say, they know what they like. What this audience liked was the "realistic" presentation of a story which seemed not to be far removed from their own experiences. What they *loved*, though, was the performance of Albert Finney. And for good reason. In his first starring role in a film Finney was nothing short of wonderful.

No doubt the highest compliment which can be paid an actor is that it is hard to imagine anyone else in a particular role. Finney simply looks and acts like Arthur Seaton should. With his short neck, jutting chin, sensual lips, puffy eyes, and cockatoo hair-do, he exhibits just the kind of aggressive vitality which sets Arthur apart. As for his acting, it simply appears perfectly natural. His role is certainly demanding, for he is asked to run a wide gamut of emotions. But that he managed to strike the proper tone every time he spoke or moved is best indicated by the response he got from a large segment of the public. This was the working-class audience, which experienced an immediate identification with Arthur. From the very start, as soon as Finney began his soliloquy at a workbench, they could recognize a temperament which "localized a whole stratum of English social class."[14]

As Brenda, Rachel Roberts is also very fine. In a role which in some ways is actually more difficult than Finney's, she always seems to have the right touch. What she does to show how Brenda moves from a naive kind of attraction for Arthur to a form of hatred mixed with pity is particularly impressive. By subtly using her expressive eyes and wide mouth, not to mention her supple voice, she ultimately projects a kind of terror of life and in the process introduces an element of genuine tragedy which enriches the film.

As for the rest of the cast, they are as a whole impressive, too. Shirley Anne Field uses her natural beauty with subtle irony to show Doreen's essential shallowness. Norman Rossington projects an authentic kind of warmth as Arthur's best friend, Bert. Hylda Baker as Aunt Ada suggests a hard-earned wisdom whenever she speaks or makes a gesture. Some of the minor figures are played by less accomplished actors. Yet even their performances have the ring of truth. For all this fine acting Reisz must be given a great deal of credit, since, as Finney himself has pointed out, he is the kind of director who works in very close collaboration with his actors.[15]

All in all, *Saturday Night* was a remarkable movie. As a matter of fact, it was so good that there are a number of critics who still feel that Reisz has not matched its artistic achievements in any of his subsequent films. Such a view doesn't really hold up in the long run. However, there is no denying the fact that in his next film there is a falling off.

3

Night Must Fall

IT IS FAIR to say that *Saturday Night and Sunday Morning* was the surprise hit of 1960 as far as most film people in Britain were concerned. One of the persons was the producer, Harry Saltzman. In admitting his own surprise, he declared that the astonishing success of the film just went to show he had always been right in suspecting that in the business of film "nobody knows anything for sure."[1] Perhaps Reisz felt like that himself as he observed how enthusiastically his first feature film was received. However, before his next film finally came out in 1964, Reisz was destined to learn that Saltzman's words could also take on a cruelly ironic meaning for him.

After *Saturday Night* came out, Reisz was suddenly one of the most prominent directors around. This, at least, was how many critics felt when they began to realize that what he had created was nothing less than a classic of British realism. Thus his next venture was eagerly awaited by many people. But what followed was not another masterpiece. Instead, it turned out to be in some ways his least satisfactory work. Needless to say, this didn't mean that Reisz had suddenly lost his "touch." He did, however, lose some of the luck which must run with a director during the course of preparing for a film.

Because of the success of *Saturday Night*, it was only natural for Reisz and Albert Finney to plan to make another movie together. The idea they came up with was to make a film about Ned Kelly, a nineteenth-century bandit who made a legend for himself in the Australian outback. This seemed to be an ideal project for them, since it promised to be an imaginative extension of their first film

47

Albert Finney at the grotesque climax of Night Must Fall

and an exciting new challenge as well. For a while, their plan was falling into place. Thus, because Reisz and Finney both wanted to make certain that their new movie would have an essential ring of authenticity, they even spent about ten weeks in Australia studying the lore of the subject and searching for the proper settings. But then they had to abandon their project when it became obvious that it simply would be too expensive for their means. The major problem was that, in order to make the film on location as they wished, they would have to deal with some difficult British labor regulations, one of which demanded that they would have to fly a large British crew to Australia. Consequently, in frustration, Reisz and Finney accepted an offer from MGM to remake the 1937 thriller *Night Must Fall*.[2]

The first version of *Night Must Fall* had been quite successful with the reviewers and the public. This was largely because of Robert Montgomery's splendid acting in the central role of Danny, an engaging psychopath. But it was also due to the fact that the film's ambition was so limited as to be rather easily fulfilled by talented people. Occasionally there are touches of psychoanalysis and social satire in the film. Mainly, however, it was meant to be simply a thriller which would keep the audience in suspense. This suspense, it must be said, was certainly of a more complex sort than is found in the run-of-the-mill melodramas of the 1930s. When Robert Montgomery first walks onto the screen, we know that his character is the killer who has cut a woman's head off, and when he arrives with a hatbox we know what is in it. We also know from the first that he is bound to murder again, probably the lady of the house where he comes to live and work. Still, because of his great charm, we don't want to believe, or even know, the dreadful truth about him. Consequently, when he murders again toward the end of the movie, and we are finally made to see the truth about him clearly, we are less shocked than disappointed. In other words, we still wish to suspend our belief in his madness, because he has been so much *fun*. And this feeling persists even at the very end, when the killer is taken off by the police, still insanely charming. The result is that, after the lights go on, we may well wonder what the point of the film was, unless it was simply to titillate us for some two hours.

Many of the most famous movies in the world, of course, are little more than simple entertainment. But given Reisz's background of concern with important issues, it was understandable that he would be reluctant to make a new version of a film which had a trifling purpose or theme to begin with. Then he thought of transforming the melodrama into a character study which would reveal certain social attitudes surrounding the killer. Perhaps in this film, as in *Saturday Night,* important concerns could after all be brought forth by focusing on a central character who is both aggressor and victim. This concept had great appeal for Finney, and thus once again, spurred by "the purest of motives and soberest of intentions," the two men set excitedly to work on their new picture.[3]

To rework the Emlyn Williams play which was the source of the original movie version, Clive Exton was brought in. At that time experiencing a growing reputation as a gifted dramatist, Exton quickly rewrote the play to try to fit it to Reisz's conceptions. He injected an understanding of what it must really feel like to be trapped on the lower class levels of the British social system. He also added a believable analysis of what motivated someone like Danny to commit murder. In the 1937 film the madman's motivations seem on occasion to be too pat. In Exton's version, however, they appear to make good sense. Danny's urge to kill has everything to do with a life of increasing despair. He strikes out because he has lost everything that used to matter, because life has continued to batter him, and because it appears to be the only way to get the respect and power he craves. To get what he wants he uses, first of all, charm. He has learned that people can be defenseless before someone who reflects their desires. And he has learned that, if they turn against him, he can get rid of them and yet keep them, too, by chopping off their heads. Of course, Danny isn't able to understand what really drives him. When he stops to try to think about what he is doing, it's hopeless. The rest of the time he is busy acting.

Problems and Flaws

One problem with *Night Must Fall* as it turned out was that while it worked rather well on the two levels of social and psychological analysis, it didn't on a third. Or, more precisely, the three levels don't quite fit together into an organic unit. That third level, melodrama, was, ironically, not meant to be of prime concern in this

film. Nevertheless, at times it clearly dominated the movie simply
because of the sensational nature of the subject matter. Exton
couldn't successfully resolve this problem in his script, although he
evidently recognized it when he told Reisz only a week before the
shooting started that they "could make a very good film if only he
didn't have to be a killer."[4] Albert Finney was even more succinct
when he tried to assess what might have gone wrong with the film.
"We meant to stick to sociology," he recalled, "but that damn head
in the hatbox proved too powerful."[5]

Related to this unresolved problem of the melodramatic element
was the acting performance of Finney. Playing Danny must have
seemed like a dream role to him at first. It was the kind which could
challenge him to the extremes of his considerable talents. In *Saturday Night* he played Arthur Seaton to perfection because he could
merge so completely with his role. In *Night Must Fall*, however,
he had the opportunity to play a character who had more than one
personality, and thus the role demanded more than identification.
It insisted on a sympathetic analysis of madness as well.

To prepare for this complex role, Finney discussed it extensively
with Reisz in advance of shooting. What was concluded was that,
for one thing, Finney would use hand and body language which
would recall his hatchet murder at the start of the film. This choppy
sort of movement would be only barely noticeable at first, but it
would intensify as the tensions which Danny felt grew. As for the
facial appearance of Danny, Finney would wear makeup to give him
a pale, waxen, slightly spectral look. But this outward appearance
was to be changed ever so slightly when the situation warranted it,
especially when we were expected to *see* the barely controlled mania
of Danny. Finally, it was determined that Finney would shift into
a clearly different performance with each of the three women who
are attracted to him in the story. Thus with the maid, pregnant with
his child, he acts like a boisterous clown. With the household's
beautiful young daughter, bored and spoiled, he is a violent lover.
With the wealthy old widow, he plays the role of the indulgent
child she would like to imagine a perfect son to be. There was also,
of course, the role of Danny when he was alone. And it was Finney's
opinion that, if his acting went wrong anywhere, it was during these
times.[6]

Actually this is true only if Finney is thinking of one such private
scene. At the very end of the movie, where the madman is pictured

Contrasting acting styles and *mise-en-scène* in two versions of Emlyn Williams's play *Night Must Fall*: (top) Dame May Whitty and Robert Montgomery as Mrs. Bramson and Danny in Richard Thorpe's dowdy, genteel 1937 version; (bottom) Albert Finney and Mona Washbourne in Karel Reisz's harsh, neurotic 1963 version.

ranting by himself, then suddenly stopping with a look of wide-eyed terror and sinking to the floor, there is a feeling that Finney, or Exton or Reisz, had a failure of imagination. First, there seems to be a gap in motivation. The look in Finney's eyes is horrific, but exactly what does he see so suddenly? We are left guessing. Then, after he sinks to the floor and begins weakly flailing out as if defending himself rather than striking at anything, we understand that this is an image of a pitiful victim. Unfortunately, Finney's choppy actions are so obviously stylized at this point that they also make us see too clearly that all this was planned to be symbolic. In short, this all-important scene ultimately lacks a spontaneous performance or quality.

In another scene Finney's acting suffers from just the opposite problem, a lack of control. This is where, just before she is murdered, the widow and Danny play a game of chase. At first Finney is perfectly believable, even delightful, as he plays the role of a "child" who is having a fine time. As the excitement grows, and Danny falls farther and farther back into childhood, however, Finney's acting gets out of hand. The scene ends with his throwing a tantrum, and Finney obviously enjoys doing this. Yet we are now too conscious of his *acting*, and thus the impression of impending dread is for a time disrupted.

Although legitimate objections to Finney's acting can be found in only these two scenes, they come at such crucial points that the damage to the film was considerable. Thus many people, evidently choosing to ignore the rest of the evidence, dismissed Finney's performance, and hence the film, as an obvious failure.

Film Style

There is no doubt that *Night Must Fall* is in certain ways Reisz's most flawed film, yet it is far from being the "disaster" that he himself once called it.[7] As a matter of fact, it is the kind of movie which bears up surprisingly well under close scrutiny because it also happens to have some of Reisz's best work in it. The way the film begins, for example, is a wonderful exercise of stylistic suggestion and economy. After an initial shot of the lovely country house where mayhem will eventually take place, the theme music, partly based on the "Three Blind Mice" melody, is heard as Olivia, the widow's daughter, comes out. It is early in the morning, the setting is perfectly peaceful and bright. Olivia, apparently lost in restlessness, moves across the garden area to the left, then to the right, where she settles on a swing. The sound of birds is heard, and as Olivia looks up, the camera follows, then falls slowly down on the nearby woods. Then it begins to track to the left, as if both looking for something and coming back toward the house. Suddenly, with the music serving as punctuation, it stops and zooms in on a man hacking away at something which is hidden from our sight by the underbrush.

Immediately after, though, there is a cut to the man first rushing with the headless body of a woman to get rid of it in a small lake, then repeating the action with an ax. As he throws the ax into the lake, it flies up high, and the camera follows it, thus recalling the preceding shot where the camera follows the upward gaze of Olivia. Next, as if to stress this ominous link, the camera cuts back to Olivia, still gently swinging and gazing, it seems, in the direction of the murder without, of course, seeing anything.

The next cut is to the widow, Mrs. Bramson, in her darkened bedroom. The fact that it is in shadow links it immediately with the only previous shadowy shot thus far, that of the decapitation in the woods. Therefore, by means of subtle lighting, we are made to suspect already that Danny's next victim may well be Mrs. Bramson rather than Olivia.

If we now start to suspect that the widow will be Danny's next target, we become rather certain of this with the very next shot. There Reisz uses a geometric arrangement which reinforces the impression that it is Mrs. Bramson who is doomed. This shot has her looking out one window from her bedroom and seeing Olivia, then looking out another and seeing the maid, Dora, arriving for work. At this point the camera not only implies a female triangle of "blind mice," but it also suggests that, because the widow is at its upended apex, she is the most vulnerable.

Hence the major lines of conflict have been introduced, and yet nothing has thus far been spoken. In the rest of the film, when words are spoken, they are often less articulate than the dynamics of formal style. Even when for once Danny talks rather freely about himself to Olivia after they have supposedly made love, the framework which contains the scene is the most eloquent part. The scene comes right after a bright, ironic episode during which Danny reads a newspaper account of the ax murder while sitting between Mrs. Bramson and her daughter. It begins at night, focusing on a police diver looking for Danny's murder weapon in the lake. As he dives once more into the perfectly black water, there is an extremely long dissolve which pictures both the air bubbles rising from the submerged diver and the bedside light in Olivia's room. Next we see that Danny is stretched out on the bed, with an entranced Olivia leaning over him and listening to what resembles a fearful confession on his part.

Danny first talks about having gone to church and seeing the death-ridden women around him. To him they were disgusting, "these great, smelly old women with their black coats and fat behinds." Then he adds that he "didn't fancy the idea of going to hell with that lot." That they were bound for hell he was quite certain, for he could imagine them, while he watched the falling of night through the colored windows, all "rotting down there" and popping "like a lot of chestnuts." As he continued his monologue, we begin to suspect that his mental illness is caused in large part by an obsessive terror of life. But we aren't really sure until after another dissolve takes place to bring the focus back on the diver.

Just before that dissolve begins, Danny points to his head and declares that he is "private." The full, complex meaning of that word becomes apparent only after the movie is over. An important aspect of its definition becomes clear, however, as we begin to see that the use of the dissolve framework is totally appropriate for the monologue. Through this means Danny's words are linked with images which express his fears better than he can. The dark lake, the diver, and the rising bubbles are all correlatives of Danny's obsessions with baptism, cleanliness, the womb, self-discovery, and death.

We might very well ask at this point why the diver must search at night. Or why, toward the very end of the movie, Olivia dares to return to the house to confront Danny after she had first run out in a panic upon seeing her decapitated mother. But Reisz's pacing throughout the film is so effective that it is only after it is over that we are likely to note these flaws in the story.

If Reisz's pacing in *Night Must Fall* is as compulsive as it was in his earlier work, it is now clearly the result of a different editing technique. Formerly, and most obviously in *Saturday Night and Sunday Morning*, Reisz elected to drive the action along by linking the scenes smoothly through various means. Now he seems often to simply chop off the top (or head?) of a scene so that we suddenly jump into the following one.

This editing style may have been influenced in part by the contemporary work of such filmmakers as Jean-Luc Godard. If it was, however, Reisz isn't using it merely because he feels like experimenting with something fashionably new. On the contrary, he has obviously settled on this tense, elliptical style because the subject of the story seems to call for it.

There are several examples of this nervous style in *Night Must Fall*, but there is one which stands out because it insinuates sexual power so well just when the story needs such an emphasis. It occurs after a scene where Olivia has been discovered by Danny poking through his room. Olivia has gone there because she is curious about the attractive new handyman, and because she thinks that Danny is at that time busy outside pushing Mrs. Bramson around in her wheelchair. When he suddenly comes in, he is at first sarcastic with her, then he soon begins to complain violently about his right to privacy. Then, after working himself into a more and more terrifying frenzy, he grabs Olivia, bends her head down to his bed, and asks her whether she likes it. For an answer, the scene cuts to Olivia riding Danny's motorbike around and around him. Obviously, Olivia's response has been in the affirmative. Reisz doesn't show us Olivia and Danny in bed together; but as she continues to ride on Danny's bike while he shouts at her to increase the power if she wishes to stay on, we can imagine all that is necessary about their sexual relationship.

By using a choppy form of editing Reisz also leaves most of the violence to our imagination. This could have been an exceedingly brutal film. Reisz, however, never has had the taste for exploiting violence. Thus we are spared from having to literally see some of the more gruesome details of Danny's story. We don't, for example, ever see the severed head which Danny carries around with him in a hatbox like a trophy. Nor do we ever actually see any of the blood which Danny causes to flow. Instead, Reisz prefers to jump quickly over Danny's grisly work to his reactions. This is totally appropriate, of course, since in this film the primary concern is with psychological matters.

It should be clear that this kind of editing strategy has its risks because so much depends on perfect timing. But, as it happens,

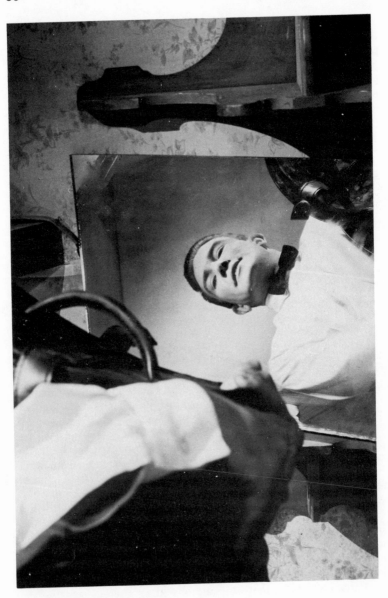

A mirror image of Danny with the notorious hatbox.

one of Reisz's obvious gifts is a fine instinct for pacing. This instinct hardly ever deserts him, and certainly not during the last half hour or so of *Night Must Fall*. If it had, that part of the movie would have collapsed. That is because it depends almost entirely on a cross-cutting structure, where the rhythm of editing is an integral part of the subject matter, both emotional and thematic.

When Reisz begins this cross-cutting sequence, it appears at first that he is choosing this technique because it creates suspense so easily and naturally. Then we soon begin to see that more is involved.

This long cross-cutting sequence starts with Olivia driving off to town after she finally begins to suspect the dangerous instability of Danny. Once she arrives there, the scene begins to switch back and forth between her and Danny. This rhythm is at first rather deliberate, but it intensifies as the awareness that Danny is about to kill Mrs. Bramson grows. Naturally, this technique is as old as the creation of suspense in movies. But Reisz adds several imaginative touches to this process.

Most obvious is his use of sound. To express the discord of Olivia's mind once she arrives in town, Reisz surrounds her with natural but highly suggestive noise. In town the street racket is deafening, and Olivia stumbles about as if she can't hear herself think. Later she goes to a movie (ironically *The Great Escape*) to get away from what thoughts do come to her. Yet inside she appears to feel subconsciously reproached as a screen voice talks about responsibility, especially toward children. Then later she is in tears while the war sounds of the movie bombard her. When she leaves the theater, there is a swelling rainstorm. Reisz manages to avoid using the rainstorm as merely a melodramatic cliché by switching from its uproar to the quietness of the house where murder is about to happen. He does this again and again, until finally the feeling is created that tempestuous noise actually means safety, and calmness, real danger.

Consequently, the fact that the scene which culminates with Mrs. Bramson's murder takes place in near silence makes it that much more frightening. Adding to this sense of terror is Reisz's reversal of another melodramatic cliché. Possibly influenced by a trick which he must have seen Hitchcock use more than once, Reisz established during the cross-cutting sequence the sense that darkness meant safety, or salvation, and light meant peril, or death. Thus by the time the widow is murdered, we are as frightened of "seeing" things as she is.

In the very last shot, Reisz's use of light is even more effective. There he uses it to express not just division but also comprehension. This shot begins with Danny haranguing about "being a madman" when crossed and about his desire to be treated with politeness. It ends with the following words by him: "I'm getting dressed now. Then we'll see what's what. Then, then we'll see. When I'm dressed. We'll see who's who. We'll see who's who." Obviously, the repetition of the word *see* is highly significant. The immediate question which the word raises is whether Danny can now really see "what's what" and "who's who." If he can't, then we at least should see that Danny is a hopelessly shattered man. That Danny is also the kind of social psychopath who sees and is seen in stark black and white terms is stressed through an interesting visual technique. By the use of gradual overexposure, or flooding of light, the last we see of Danny is turned into a haunting picture. As the light grows, Danny seems to become more and more set off from his surroundings by sharp lines of contrast, and more and more like a strange abstraction of light and dark. Finally, we can begin to imagine that from his point of view he feels more and more clearly exposed to dangerous forces while at the same time, as the light continues to pour in, he can literally see us and our world less and less clearly in the glare.

It should be evident by now that throughout *Night Must Fall* Reisz tries to employ a style so that the way we are made to see certain things is all important. Thus, for example, it is no mere flamboyancy on his part when Reisz uses the zoom shot again and again. Actually, he seems to use it with three results in mind. First, it is the kind of shot which may signify discovery, revelation, and surprise. These are, as has been shown, all important elements of the film. In addition, when used with a certain sense of rhythm, they can have a sexual implication. Obviously, sex is on Danny's mind. Finally, the zoom can suggest violence. Appropriately enough, the first time we discover Danny at his gruesome job, the camera zooms in. When he is about to kill again, the zoom is reversed. This time, as the camera eye is yanked back suddenly, two subliminal, psychological effects are left on the viewer. First, when the reverse zoom occurs as the widow stumbles away from the advancing Danny toward us, we can feel her helpless panic almost sensually because the perspective seems to rush directly at us.

Second, we can feel the threat of Danny more directly because the whole scene, or the camera eye, is pulled back so violently that it seems to be driving, or aiming, at *us*. Needless to say, these are precisely the kinds of unsettling thoughts Reisz has in mind for us. Paranoia is the proper response at this point.

The discerning viewer should also respond to some of the many symbolic things which are found in the death house. It holds many round objects, suggestive of both sex and decapitation. On the walls in the hall hang strange head pictures which serve as reminders of Danny's trophy in his hatbox. These heads, in profile and in relief, also imply that a character study is underway. To stress this analytical point, and the related one that there are people in the house who are blind to themselves and to others, several mirrors are used. To indicate Danny's entrapment, he is often shot through the bars of windows or a banister or with a low, beamed ceiling over him. That he is fascinated with penetration is implied by the way he handles various pointed objects. The list could go on.

Indeed, the discussion of the admirable aspects of the movie might go on at some length. Much, for instance, could be said about the fine performances of Mona Washbourne as Mrs. Bramson, Susan Hampshire as Olivia, and Sheila Hancock as Dora. However, one would still have to come back to the question of why the picture was so poorly received by the public and the critics. Of course, there are the film's flaws which have already been mentioned. But that is actually only part of the answer.

The Film's Reception

It is easy to see why at the box office *Night Must Fall* didn't do as well as *Saturday Night*. The members of the popular audience certainly weren't going to identify eagerly with the character Albert Finney was portraying this time. Nor would they be very interested in Reisz's complex stylistics, which seemed to some viewers to result in a muddled thriller. As for the various critical reviews, it has to be concluded that a number of them were written with a strong nostalgia for the 1937 version of the picture. Others merely focused on the flaws of Finney's performance, ignoring the rest. Still others responded to the film with impatience or severe disappointment because, it appeared to them, Reisz had deliberately turned away

from social realism. Seeing this as a form of betrayal, these critics
in particular at times staggered Reisz with heated accusations that
he was "selling out" and "going commercial."[8]

Another source of violent criticism was perhaps the most personally discouraging to Reisz. This came from an influential segment
of the female audience who objected to Finney's being cast in such
a jarring role as Danny's to begin with. As Reisz recalls, "All the
wives at MGM who had seen the star as Tom Jones, adoring him,
rounded on me like avenging Furies screaming, 'What have you
done to this beautiful boy?' " Their impression was that Finney had
been terribly misused by being cast in an "unsympathetic role,"
and however shallow such a conception was, it was damaging to
Reisz.[9]

Film politics being what they are, first impressions are all important, whatever the sources—the public, the reviewers, or even
the wives of film executives. Consequently, after *Night Must Fall*
came out, the feeling quickly spread that the movie was a failure
in more ways than one. Thus Reisz suddenly found that he was no
longer one of the unmistakably "hot" directors of British cinema.
Before he could undergo a critical rehabilitation, he would have to
make another important and successful film. Fortunately, his next
picture answered these demands.

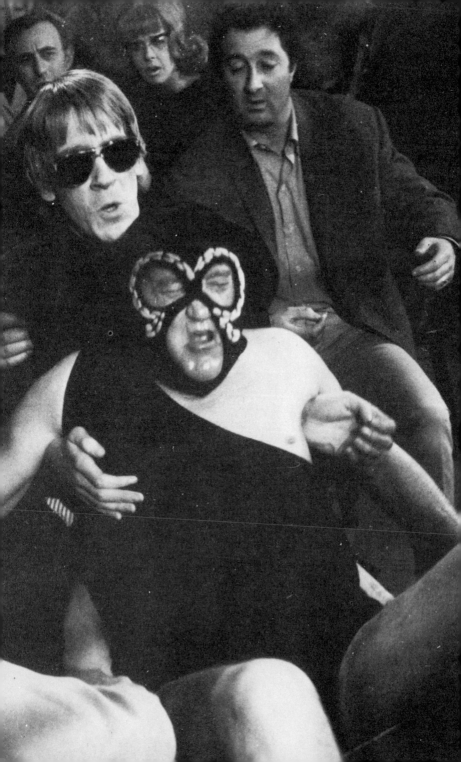

4

Morgan!

THE PRESSURES on a filmmaker to conform for the sake of box-office success are bound to be enormous wherever commercial movies are made. In Britain, however, the filmmaker is more vulnerable than most of his counterparts in other countries because of certain established conservative forces. There, as Roger Manvell describes it, he is constantly faced with the pressure to conform not only commercially but also "to conform to the censorship, to conform politically, to conform socially and not offend pressure-groups with particular influence. Above all, perhaps, the pressure on him is to be consistently successful, never to make a film which will send him back to square one in his career, or ditch him altogether."[1] Thus after what was widely perceived to be the failure of *Night Must Fall*, it was rather daring of Reisz to come out with a film about two years later which was so unusual that it seemed to be completely out of step with the conventional box-office movie.[2] This was *Morgan!*, an intense comedy inspired by the subject of insanity.

Like *Night Must Fall*, it centers on a person who is mad. But the difference is that, while Danny is driven mad with hatred, Morgan Delt is driven mad with love. He loves flowers, animals, children, political exiles, any living thing which is good or beautiful or is in need of sympathetic protection. Above all, he loves his wife, Leonie. Unfortunately for Morgan, she wants to divorce him and marry an art dealer by the name of Napier. To keep her from doing so, Morgan tries an assortment of increasingly wild and desperate schemes. As his desperation grows, so does his imagined identification with a gorilla, an animal he is especially fond of because it is "big, but good." Finally, when this identification is complete, he

63

David Warner in one of many predicaments during Morgan!

loses not only Leonie but his hold on sanity as well. However, the epilogue of the film suggests that, in a way, Morgan has won. In the end, Leonie is pregnant with his baby, and his most important instincts seem still to be alive.

To the surprise of many, *Morgan!* quickly became very popular. In fact, it became a kind of a cult film with the young. What was it about the movie that held such an attraction for them? Most obviously, they loved what the central character and the spirit of the film stood for. Good films are not made in a vacuum, and *Morgan!* is quintessentially of its time, the 1960s. In Britain that was the age of the Beatles, hippies, and youthful rebellion as a whole. The film reflects this atmosphere, and the central character embodies many of its beliefs, however eccentric, naive, or sentimental they may be. Morgan was a nonconformist, a dreamer, a romantic anarchist in conflict with conventional society. To the young, he thus appeared to be one of them. That he actually goes insane in the end didn't really seem to disturb them, because he looked like he was happy to be in that state, and perhaps because taking leave of one's senses seemed to be not exactly an ironic, but certainly a crafty way of escaping the restraints of society.

In this connection, Alex Walker appears to be correct when he claims that *Morgan!* was "probably the first film of social protest to be adopted as their own by the post-Porter generation, the teenagers who had been children in 1959. And in this sense, it was a prophetic film. It was one of the earliest appearances in the commercial cinema of the kid who feels an outcast" and who, in the jargon of the 1960s, consequently decides to simply "drop out."[3] Needless to say, the film was unpopular with many of the viewing public precisely because it had such a protagonist. This was especially true of the older film public, but by no means limited to them. Anyone who disliked the period or its youth culture was bound to dislike *Morgan!* and perhaps even hate it, for it was the type of film which was naturally going to inspire very strong reactions one way or the other.

Critical Response

Certainly this was true of the critics. Thus, for instance, Dwight MacDonald complained at length about the many flaws which he found in *Morgan!* and finally decided that it was "a mess, a very up-to-date Carnaby Street mod mess. . . . "[4] Brendan Gill, on the other hand, wrote that Reisz was deserving of very high praise "for the force and courage of his direction."[5] The critics who didn't simply hate or love the movie were few and far between. One was Pauline Kael.

In her review of *Morgan!* it seems clear that her first impulse must have been to lambaste it for its flaws. Then her curiosity about its impact on so many of the young was aroused. Hence her conclusion was that if it was a bad movie, this was really "a minor matter. The point is that it's not an ordinary movie and whether it's good or bad is of less interest than why so many young people respond to it the way they do, especially as, in this case, they are probably responding to exactly what we think makes it bad. Sometimes bad movies are more important than good ones just because of those unresolved elements that make them such a mess. They may get at something going on around us that the moviemakers felt or shared and expressed in a confused way."[6] To her mind, she then continued in her review, the people who made this film found a common bond with their youthful audience when, like them, they decided to *accept* the confusion of the material. And this "indifference to artistic control" was something new.[7]

It is a measure of Kael's critical influence that her view of *Morgan!* seems today to have become the prevailing one. And yet, although she may have been correct about the young people's indifference to artistic form in *Morgan!*, she was certainly wrong to ascribe such an attitude to Reisz and his collaborators. The truth is that Reisz has never worked on a film without practicing the greatest kind of artistic control. It's simply not in his nature to make films without considered, methodical patterns and forms. Consequently, when there are noticeable flaws in his films they are usually the result not of indifference but of his intense passion for perfect artistic order. That is, at times his movies lack a certain spontaneity, or life, because it becomes too obvious that someone is trying ever so carefully to manipulate things for particular effects. *Morgan!* is no exception. There are flaws in the film, and they are mostly caused by Reisz's formulaic impulse. But, just as in all of his pictures, it is this same impulse which is also mainly responsible for the best parts.

Humor and Film Technique

Much of the best humor of *Morgan!*, for example, actually derives less from the script than from this formulaic impulse. To extract as much humor out of the story as possible, Reisz seemed to take his own advice. In *The Technique of Film Editing* he had written that when making a comedy "it is often not necessary to convince the spectator of anything; it is only necessary to make him laugh. If this involves a harsh cut, a faulty piece of continuity or any other unrealistic distortion, then that may be all to the good. The funniest films are often those in which the editor has been absolutely ruthless in his disregard for reality and concentrated solely on extracting the maximum of humour out of every situation."[8] When the story of Morgan called for humor, Reisz indeed was "ruthless" in his editing. He also took very great risks with the planning of some of the humorous scenes. To his credit, with rare exceptions, his risks paid off.

Reisz creates some of his most successful humor through the use of sound effects, but mostly it results from the use of visual surprise and incongruity. Time and time again, what we see strikes us with its inventive wit. Of course, this form of wit is also derivative. For the kind of visual humor which Reisz employs goes back to the silent comedy years. Thus on occasion watching *Morgan!* is something like watching a nostalgic tribute to the films of Mack Sennett. Certainly many of the visual techniques used by Reisz were a standard part of those old movies. There is a great deal of slapstick action, shot at a frenzied pace, sometimes even in fast motion. There are chase scenes, pratfalls, and practical jokes. There are bobbies who resemble Keystone Kops. Above all, there are the scenes where Morgan is planning ever more desperate tricks to win back Leonie. Each time he tries something new, we first see him laying the groundwork, and thus we know what to expect. But then we are forced to wait for the anticipated result. As we wait, we hold our breath, as it were, with laughter. It's a trick which all the great silent comedy stars knew. It's a trick which still works very well, as this film shows.

Perhaps the least clearly understood aspect of *Morgan!* is that its humor has a purpose behind the laughter. Mostly, it is meant as social satire. Not surprisingly, most of this satire is aimed at the forces which are in active opposition to Morgan's way of life. Thus the workers who are busy rebuilding Leonie's house into an apartment complex are compared to monkeys at one point. The modern artworks found in Napier's gallery seem especially silly when they are compared with what Morgan prefers to paint, beautiful or powerful animals. They are cold, sharp forms which are certainly not hurt, and might even be helped, by a stray bullet from a gun which goes off by accident in Napier's hands. As far as Morgan is concerned, Napier's kind of art is also especially useful to hide behind when he is being chased. The police, of course, are marked for special attention, and come out looking exceedingly silly. A constable, for instance, is seen playing hopscotch, then shifting his derriere toward the camera in close-up as a voice from Morgan's radio says "Good morning!" Then the courts, too, are made to look foolish. One lawyer is simply stunned by what to him seems a particularly heinous thing for Morgan to do, to shave a hammer and sickle on Leonie's dog. For once, words appear to fail him. As for the rest of the "sane" people in the film, they are mostly made to look rather absurd, too.

It might be argued that since what is mocked seems preferable to the apparent alternative in the film (that is, "insanity" as represented by Morgan) then consequently the satire is really not effectual, or serious, or even satire in the strict sense of the word. That, in other words, it isn't pure satire because it isn't clearly poised against a norm which is obviously rational. This is true, as far as it goes. Within the movie, there indeed are no clear choices between the foolish and the reasonable. Thus we have to go outside to find the source of good sense; that is, to Reisz himself. It is he who finds the forces opposing Morgan so absurd. But—and this is extremely germane—he finds Morgan somewhat absurd, too. As a result, the film is a satire in a wide sense of the word, a satire trained on some of the absurdities which Reisz sees residing in human nature as a whole.

Reisz indicates that he may have been drawn to Morgan in the first place for a personal reason when he says that the "character seemed very relevant to me since I had had a left-wing youth myself in Czechoslovakia, an allegiance swiftly broken by the Soviet-inspired purges there in 1947–50."[9] He denies, however, that Morgan is any more a spokesman for him than was Arthur Seaton. Instead, what he finally saw in Morgan was a kind of saintly fool with a "divine spark which provoked the question of who is mad and who

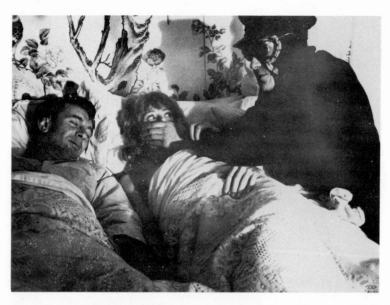

David Warner as Morgan Delt plays a series of grisly pranks on his estranged wife
Leonie (Vanessa Redgrave) and (top) her lover Napier (Robert Stephens), often
involving what he considers their sullied marital bed.

is sane, analogous to the way our older generation treats today's hippies as freaks, as 'cases.' The film seemed to me a way to bridge the generations."[10] Apparently he felt that one way to bridge the generation gap was to make both sides look rather foolish, with the hope that neither one would take itself so seriously thereafter. Hence he felt free, particularly in the earlier part of the film, to make Morgan the target of some of his satire, too. If he subsequently makes less and less fun of Morgan, this is evidently because he wishes to stress the point that, if Morgan can be as absurd as anybody else, he is also really heading toward a serious mental breakdown.

Appropriate Style and Key Scenes

Although this process of disintegration is written into the script, it is characteristic of Reisz that he chose to use a film style which derives from and emphasizes Morgan's character and condition. Of course, this gave the movie a look which some critics have called eccentric, messy, or simply chaotic. To call it a shifting, nervous, stream-of-consciousness style seems more precise, however, and to the point. Morgan's world and mind are falling apart, and the film's style often allows us to see this most clearly. At other times, particularly before Morgan's mental condition reaches an obviously critical state, the style is appropriately riotous or ironic. This stylistic quality is illustrated, for example, in an early scene which takes place in Napier's gallery. Having found out that Napier has gone so far as to sleep with Leonie in her own bed, not to mention keeping his toothbrush in her bathroom, Morgan enters the gallery with gun in hand, threatening the man's life. Napier disarms him in his office by simply exchanging the gun in Morgan's hand with a drinking glass. But Morgan then puts on brass knuckles. Still, Napier is unflappable, even after the gun which he is carelessly handling goes off accidentally. Morgan, after all, may be crazy, but he is certainly not to be taken seriously. He is just a pest, Napier believes.

In this frame of mind, Napier leaves the unhappy husband to brood for a while in his office. At this time Morgan, having been in the meantime also disarmed of his brass knuckles by the composed Napier, pulls out a switch-blade knife. Then Reisz uses a wipe, which suggests not only a passage of time but also, in a comic way, what is on Morgan's mind—to wipe Napier off the face of the earth.

When Napier returns to his office to find that Morgan is still there, he becomes somewhat impatient. Finally he gives Morgan the facts of the situation. As he puts it, Morgan will simply have to adjust to the reality that Leonie is through with him and that she now loves Napier and is ready to marry him. This is too much for Morgan. He leaps for Napier's throat. Because this is now shot in fast motion, the action doesn't appear violent at all, only farcical. After all, Morgan is no killer, just a fool in love.

Napier manages to push the alarm button while Morgan is clinging to and shaking his throat, and in the next shot Morgan is pictured being chased about through the gallery. Also shown in fast motion, with the addition of a sound effect which suggests the patter of little feet, all of the participants look thoroughly absurd, like wound-up toys. The game ends suddenly when Morgan is caught by the scruff of his neck while he is peeking through a piece of modern art which is actually a metallic eyesore. As he is tossed out on the sidewalk, he protests that he is not through with Napier. However, as if to tell us that he is really all done, cooked, the very next shot is a close-up of eggs frying in a pan.

In a later scene where Morgan takes his mother to Karl Marx's gravesite, Reisz's sense of the ridiculous is also made apparent through some visual irony, but in a somewhat less hectic manner this time. This shift is totally appropriate because Morgan feels so much calmer and safer when he is with his mother. Hence the scene begins with the camera slowly lifting up from an epitaph beneath Marx's formidable stone face. For a moment it's like seeing a mirror image of an earlier scene. In that previous scene, Morgan put his stuffed gorilla on the left side of the screen, facing the camera, looking like it was standing guard over his studio. Now Marx stares at us from the right side of the screen with his gorillalike countenance. It is a neat way of ironically comparing the stuffed gorilla with the philosopher, and to make us see that Morgan's obsession with gorillas may actually go as far back as his youthful infatuation with the ideology propounded by Marx.

This scene ends with Marx still looking at us gravely, but in the background Morgan is now carrying his sore-footed mother piggy-back while crying out, "Up the revolution!" Poor Marx; this seems hardly the way one of his anniversaries should be celebrated. On the other hand, perhaps it is fitting, even if farcical. It is, after all, a picture of a member of the working class helping another worker, and of a man literally burdened with the weight of his heritage.

There are many such examples of Reisz's cunning style in the film as a whole. But the best examples can be found in those scenes where we follow Morgan's mental disintegration coupled with his growing belief in fantasy, especially in his identification with gorillas.

The first sounds we hear, before we actually see anything of the movie, are those of a gorilla. Then we see a mid-shot of Morgan. He is listening to a recording which is describing the life and character of a gorilla. While he is doing so, the camera moves toward his very attentive face. Thus we already see that Morgan is especially drawn to gorillas, and we hear why this is so. The recording tells us, among other things, that the gorilla has no natural enemies and is an enemy to no one, but that if an adult male is made angry, he is a formidable sight. That if he is surprised "by an intruder, he will tear down great branches, roar his anger, and beat his chest." These recorded words, as the viewer will soon discover, are like the forewords to the action.

Reisz does some other interesting things in this introductory scene to stress Morgan's deep fascination with gorillas. Just before the credits begin, there is the loud clanging sound of a metal door opening. Morgan turns his head toward the sound, and there is a gorilla coming into his cage. Morgan presses against the glass of the cage to get a closer look. Then, while the credits continue, Reisz cuts back and forth between Morgan and the gorilla, in close-up, looking at each other. As a result, the reflective connection between the two is strengthened, to the point where one senses that Morgan may be even thinking that he is seeing *himself* in the cage. To emphasize even more these first impressions that the film will be a kind of "portrait" of a schizoid, Reisz uses several quick freeze shots of Morgan staring into the cage.

In the next scene, Morgan is first seen in long shot walking jauntily toward us. Then when he arrives at his, or actually Leonie's, house, he sees several men on scaffoldings working on the building. As he looks up at them, the camera moves toward him to the point where he is in close-up, and suddenly there is a cut to a monkey swinging from limb to limb. It's a startling cut, but totally appropriate for the subject at hand. It's the way Morgan's mind works, after all. First, because he is an artist, he sees, or imagines, things in a sharply visual way. Second, and more ominously, his mind is in such a state that it shifts immediately from reality to fantasy. To him there doesn't seem to be a real difference.

In this scene, of course, Morgan's vision of the workers is ironic. And so are his subsequent visions which concern other people. For instance, his "seeing" a beautiful girl as a peacock, a yawning fat man as a hippo, and his mother-in-law as an eagle. As for his fantasizing during the first love scene with Leonie, it is full of charm and enchantment. While she lies in bed waiting for him to undress, he looks down and pictures her first as a zebra rolling in ecstasy on the ground, then as a lioness. And once they begin making love, Reisz cross-cuts between them and two zebras going through a mating ritual, then ends the scene with a shot of two birds flying off together.

Morgan's purely personal fantasies, however, although they may be quite funny and charming in the first part of the film, get increasingly more serious and sad. Thus when he has his first vision of a gorilla, we have to smile. When he looks through his studio window, down to the little garden area behind the house, he "sees" a gorilla looking up. As their eyes appear to meet, the gorilla beats his chest and Morgan smiles. They understand each other, they seem to be saying.

Morgan's next gorilla vision starts out happily, but it ends on a rather ominous note. As a matter of fact, it is a dream vision, for it occurs while he is sleeping in a car which is parked outside Leonie's house like a siege. At any rate, he seems very happy while he is having the dream. His ultimate dream, of course, is to get Leonie back. The way his actual dream ends, however, appears to emphasize the futility of that hope, and of more. In the dream vision, the gorilla is happily, gracefully swinging through the trees. Then suddenly the overlapping sound of an alarm clock goes off, and the gorilla lets go of a limb and falls, literally, down and off the screen as if into oblivion. No wonder that, when a cut to Morgan's face in close-up follows, he seems reluctant to stir from his dream and face the morning. The dream, and the alarm sound, appear to be warnings about the real world.

As the real world finally and literally begins to close in on Morgan, his fantasies become more and more pronounced, with predictable results. After Morgan's desperation reaches the point at which he and a friend (appropriately a wrestler known as Wally the Gorilla) kidnap Leonie, the law steps in. Before that actually happens, Morgan does imagine that, having taken Leonie by force, he may have solved his problems after all. Thus he can have one of his most extended, and extreme, fantasies. He pictures himself as Tarzan, frolicking in the water with his girl, then saving her from an alligator. During this fantasizing, Reisz does a wonderful bit of cross-cutting, in the process showing just how comic yet enchanting Morgan's vision was, and ultimately how sad.

When the visionary experience is over, Morgan's situation is more hopeless than ever. Now even he realizes it. At least he does so for the time being. That is why he tells Leonie just how lonely and frightened he feels. Leonie responds to this desperate expression of his love for her, and they fall to the ground in an embrace. That she will now remain his, however, is just a dream. Soon reality crashes into the picture.

To express this transition from fantasy to fact, Reisz does some extremely imaginative things. As Morgan and Leonie fall to the ground and begin to make love, the scene is overexposed, making it look as if it's simply flooded with light. Also, the love scene is shot in what might be called pixillated slow motion, thus giving it an especially enchanting, magical quality. Finally, the camera pulls back slowly while the love scene goes on, and then, when it is in long shot, it pans to the right. Suddenly, with the style now appearing to be strictly realistic, the camera picks up a car driving by. It is the car which has come to rescue Leonie, representing in effect the outside, the real world, closing in on Morgan.

To put it another way, when the car arrives Morgan's game is up, and as a consequence he next finds himself in court. There, while charges are being read against him, Morgan has his next vision. Placed in the bottom right-hand corner of the screen, thus making him seem especially vulnerable, he imagines seeing some giraffes being hunted down. Significantly, this vision is pictured in superimposition, since Reisz evidently wishes to stress the fact that for Morgan the distinction between reality and fantasy seems no longer to clearly exist. Also significantly, Morgan ends up smiling when in his imagination the giraffes escape. Perhaps to him it's as if he is destined to escape, too. But if that is really on his mind, it's a futile thought.

In the next scene, Morgan is driven up to jail. He still thinks it's a lark and, while the police trip over each other behind him, he runs toward the jail's door and dives in. When the door slams shut behind him, we are bound to laugh. But it is actually the last real laugh we will have, until possibly the very last part of the movie. Following this shot the mood of the film changes noticeably.

After a fade, the next shot begins with the camera sitting exactly where it sat at the end of the previous one; but when Morgan comes out, he acts very differently. When the jail door is closed behind him, he begins to run from it. And as the camera moves toward him at the same time, we can see the worried, wounded look on his face. We can only imagine what was literally done to him in jail. We can surmise, however, that because of that experience he has truly lost his hold on his sanity.

After the next scene, there is certainly no doubt of this. It's a pivotal scene which, though short and plain and presented without a word spoken, is very expressive of Morgan's condition. It begins with Morgan in his old, bare studio unpacking a gorilla outfit. He puts on the head, crawls at first toward a mirror, and then stands up to look at himself. The slanted mirror, the eerie music, and Morgan's soft gorillalike sounds which he makes while flexing the mouth of the mask all add up to a bizarre, haunting image. After what seems like an interminable moment, compounding the feeling that he is truly transfixed by his reflection, Morgan walks back to the same spot where he was when the scene began, sits down, and looks toward the camera. As he sits and looks toward us, we may notice that there are intervening pillars to suggest imprisonment. In other words, we may at this point suspect that Morgan's condition is now similar to that of the caged gorilla he was looking at at the start of the film. Because *Morgan!* is generally a noisy film, we are also bound to notice that the silence which engulfs him is profound. All this, significantly shot in one take, clearly shows that Morgan has now reached the point where he is trapped by his fantasies. To punctuate this fact, just before the scene ends we suddenly hear a monstrous roar.

This is, appropriately enough, coming from the most famous of all "gorilla movies," *King Kong*. Morgan is now at a theater watching it, smiling and shaking his head with admiration while the monster roars away. That Morgan's fantasizing has reached the point where he not only identifies himself with gorillas in general, but with The

Gorilla, is now stressed by Reisz through the means of a short sequence of shots. From a picture of King Kong on the theater screen, Reisz cuts to a close-up of Morgan looking on with approval. A close-up of the gorilla follows, and then there is a dissolve from the monster's face to Morgan in the head of his gorilla suit. Now the camera begins to move in even closer, until in extreme close-up we can see Morgan's eyes looking for something as they move. The next shot, a pan shot, suggests what that is. The shot moves across part of the skyline and stops on top of a building where Leonie's wedding party is taking place. This is Morgan's next, and last, target which he is going to assault with his desperate love.

After the camera moves about the light-flooded party scene for a brief time, it suddenly looks down from the top, seems to move right through the trees below, and discovers Morgan. Significantly, this was the point of view which Morgan himself was seen to have during his first gorilla vision. As Morgan looks up to the party, Reisz cuts to a shot of King Kong looking up a skyscraper's side before he starts to climb it. Then, after Morgan finds himself on top of the building and crashes the party, there are several more cross-cuts between him and the monster.

Morgan is successful in ruining the party, of course, but it doesn't really solve any of his problems. On the contrary, he finds that he consequently has to make a run for his life—literally. For while he is chased by two of the irate members of the party, his gorilla suit catches on fire (something which was foreshadowed, incidentally, since his stuffed gorilla had caught fire earlier in the story). To put the fire out, the only thing he can finally think to do is swipe a motorcycle and head for the river.

The sequence which follows is especially well planned by Reisz. As Morgan roars off on the cycle, his desperate and absurd condition is emphasized through a number of stylistic choices. When he is first seen racing along in heavy traffic, we can pick out Morgan because, although an extremely long high angle shot is used, he has become a cloud of smoke. When, subsequently, we get a closer look of him, we are struck less by the absurdity of a smoking gorilla on a cycle than the sadness of a crazed human being.

To stress his disorientation and frenzy, Reisz now uses some wide angle distortions, criss-cross patterns of direction, and shifts in the film's speed. He also has us hear Morgan's sounds of terror—and that is all they are, sounds. Finally, when the cycle flies up and off a ramp and Morgan falls into the water, his cry of relief is like the moan of a wounded animal.

After Morgan falls into the water, there is a long fade. The next thing we see is Morgan's gorilla face in extreme close-up, looking beaten and dazed. This image introduces us to what is about to follow—a surrealistic death vision. Just before that vision begins, Morgan slips and falls over and into piles of metal junk. The scene is evidently a factory scrapyard, and it looks like a perfect image of the industrial world which Morgan abhors. As he stumbles about, he tries to pull off his gorilla mask, ever more desperately. Finally, lying in a heap of empty cans, he wrenches it off. As he does, Reisz combines a freeze shot and a dissolve to perfectly capture Morgan's stunned, confused, and dislocated state of mind. During the course of this vision, the film overexposed to give it a nightmarish quality, Morgan is made to confront in a symbolic way the various fears and pressures which have been driving him crazy. They are so overwhelming that he finally sees himself shot down by a small army of men who surround him, and by Leonie, who sends the final bullets into him from a submachine gun.

If, in Morgan's schizoid mind, one of him is now dead, who is left? The answer is predictable. As he is loaded into an ambulance after his mental ordeal, he feels the arms of the gorilla suit which he is still wearing on his body, and he says happily, "I've become all furry." This is, of course, what he has wanted for some time now. It is also what lands him in an asylum, where the next and final scene takes place.

The Final Scene and Its Imagery

Typical of Reisz, the penultimate scene is somewhat ambiguous. It begins simply enough, with a long tracking shot of Leonie, now pregnant, coming to see Morgan in the asylum. We must note, however, as we follow along with Leonie, that she has entered an extraordinary place. It looks paradisiacal, flooded with light, trees and flowers everywhere, and seemingly very contented people all about. When we see Morgan, he looks very content, too, as he works in a flowerbed. When he sees Leonie, a freeze shot of him suggests a momentary recognition of what he has loved and lost.

But then he turns back to his flowers, as if by conscious choice. He is a few moments later briefly roused by the news that, indeed, Leonie is carrying his baby, and then again by her ironic laughter. That her world, however, and his are really two completely different ones now, and that this is fine with him, is emphasized stylistically through two more short freeze shots of Morgan and through some rhythmic, contrasting close-ups between him and Leonie. Thus, after her laughter runs down, Leonie has nothing else to do but either look at Morgan's back bending over his flowers or leave. She leaves, naturally, and as she gets up to go the camera lifts up with her. And then it continues to rise up and up, until we have a long bird's-eye view of Morgan working in his garden bed, then joyously leaping over a part of his creation. It is a flower arrangement of a hammer and sickle.

What was one to make of this last image? The evidence has it that the youthful part of the audience just responded with instinctive laughter. Many other people, however, felt that they had to agonize over this final image, and many of them came to obviously the wrong conclusions. Among them was the predictable, simplistic, reflex conclusion that the last image was meant as a kind of personal, ideological call to arms. This view can be dismissed by noting what Reisz said and implied about Morgan's attraction to communism and its symbolism. Morgan, he thought, was a type of person who "has a nursery full of idealistic and ideological toys: it could have been crucifixes, it just happened to be Lenin and Trotsky. . . . It seems to be extremely germane to the way young people are now."[11] As a rule, of course, young people are idealistic and politically naive. In the 1960s they were also *eager* to shock their more conservative elders, and thus were very fond of all sorts of revolutionary symbolism. Therefore, the final hammer and sickle image isn't meant to have any serious political implications. It's simply there to tell us that Morgan's rebellious spirit is still young and alive.

Another interpretation of the final image, that it is just imposed on the film to get a last laugh out of the audience, can be dismissed with basically the same line of reasoning used in the previous paragraph. It can also be dismissed by bringing up the fact that this image has been a recurrent one in the film, and that it functions as one of the organic symbols of Morgan's defiant spirit every time. Thus even if, as Pauline Kael claims, this last image has been borrowed from the end of Luis Buñuel's *El*, it fits into the total scheme

Morgan finds peace at last with a pregnant Leonie in the garden of the madhouse

of the movie. It doesn't simply, as she puts it, supply a "larky" conclusion.[12] It *punctuates* the film. Based on the evidence of the rest of his movies, it seems obvious that this is what Reisz must have in mind.

That doesn't mean that the film's epilogue is totally successful. The one thing which doesn't work well at all is Leonie's protracted laughter. Why does it have to last so long, and what is it really supposed to mean? It is obviously supposed to *mean* something important because of its unnatural length and because of its unusual, echoic quality. One feels that the news that Morgan has indeed impregnated Leonie may be funny to her, but not *that* funny. Instead, the real point seems to be that Reisz thinks it's perfectly wonderful news, and he wishes to make certain that we understand its ironic meaning correctly. The thing is that we are bound to feel like laughing ourselves without, as it were, Leonie's canned laughter. It is surely a delectable turn of events, and a wonderfully symbolic one as well, since this means that the "crazy" line of Morgan will apparently continue. Thus, for once, Reisz is somewhat lacking in subtlety. The worst thing about this forced laughter is not that it is banal, however. It may also be distracting in a very serious way. As one critic puts it, it runs the risk of laughing "the point away."[13]

Questions of Theme

What, then, is the point, or theme, of the movie, one might still ask. The answer, naturally, is not simple. However, as the last image of the film suggests, it is mainly a rebellious one. What really matters in this picture is what Morgan is against, and what he *does* about it, as opposed to what *happens* to him.

Morgan goes insane. That is what happens to him. It isn't what he chooses, even if that is what many of the young viewers apparently preferred to believe.[14] What he chooses to do, and continually tries to do with less and less success, is to counter those forces which are generally called "normal." To him they seem like forms of assault. When the "normal" forces, in the person of Napier, even threaten to take Leonie away from him, he decides to fight back.

To see that this is the real case we can recall the path that his madness takes and the social forces (invariably satirized) which meet him along the way. We also have his words at two key points in the movie. In the first, a constable has warned him that, when Morgan playfully daubed him with a bit of shaving cream on the nose, it was, "technically speaking," a form of assault. To this Morgan responds: "Is there anything which isn't an assault, technically speaking? Birth, sex, work, life, death." The befuddled constable answers that Morgan just ought "to watch it." "Yeah, I know," says Morgan. "But where is it?"

This might sound rather like paranoia on Morgan's part, but that would be ignoring what happens in the rest of the picture. Again and again "it," or the force of the "normal" way of doing things, is there ready to confront him. What is wonderful about Morgan is that, in a fundamental way, he isn't beaten. Therefore, in the words of David Mercer, who wrote the script based on his own teleplay, *Morgan!* is "about a human being under stress and about the manner in which he ultimately preserves his integrity against society."[15]

The ultimate manner in which he chooses to preserve that integrity is, of course, withdrawal. That he thinks there is no other choice is indicated by his "last words" before he sees himself executed during his death vision. "All that is holy is profaned," he says. Given this fact, the world of imagination seems to be the only possible one for him. He crosses into that world willingly, it seems. Up to a point, therefore, the film encourages the world of imagination as a form of salvation. Unfortunately, taking such a step, if it is radical enough, is destined to bring a human being not only a sort of freedom but also insanity.

Problems and Flaws

Mainly because the line between Morgan's choosing unreality and his becoming insane is rather fine, there has been, as we have seen, some confusion about the film's true point. Whether or not this should be consequently seen as a real flaw in the film depends, it seems, on the way one looks at film as art. If one sees film as an art form which is naturally a medium that makes a direct and unambiguous statement, it would appear to be a flaw. If one sees film as an art which should move toward abstraction and ambiguity, it wouldn't. In any case, it is a "problem" which exists in the movie.

Morgan! has some other problems which should be pointed out even if they aren't very serious. One is the fact that, after the gravity of Morgan's mental condition becomes quite apparent, there is occasionally comedy which isn't totally appropriate. Most obviously, there are too many cross-cuts between King Kong and Morgan when he crashes Leonie's wedding party. We are already so aware of his identification with the monster by this time that it's not necessary to have flash shots of King Kong, for example, looking through a skyscraper window at a pair of lovers, or growling in front of a tied up Fay Wray, or of his beating his chest in front of her. These shots actually detract from the seriousness of Morgan's feelings, giving a somewhat campy flavor to the scene.

One can find fault with Morgan's surrealistic death vision, too. Reisz seems to have had too great ambitions for it. If one analyzes it closely enough, it has all of the appropriate symbolic pieces which fit the puzzle of Morgan's fears and obsessions. The problem is, however, that some of this symbolism is bound to escape the ordinary or inexperienced viewer because it comes upon him so suddenly and with such weight. Thus it isn't difficult to imagine the young audience in particular thinking that this was all so "weird," and letting it go at that.

A final problem is the performance of Vanessa Redgrave in the role of Leonie. Actually, the problem is more a question of casting than acting. Redgrave is extremely talented—in fact, a great film actress, as she certainly proves in Reisz's next film. However, she just appears to be wrong for the part. She seems too elegant and too composed. In other words, she isn't zany or nutty enough for this mad picture. When she tries to act like everyone else in it, it simply doesn't work very well.

This is true even if she did win the Cannes Film Festival best actress award for her work. And it's also true even if her memories of working in the film are such happy ones. As she recalls, in *Morgan!* she "worked for the first time with people who made films as films should be made." She had come off a confusing film acting experience, but Reisz "explained to me that in filming each individual scene is a whole unit, and its own value must be found, unlike a play which has a single value and climbs to it from start to finish." To get her properly into the role, she recalls, they "rehearsed a bit too. I was very nervous and I overacted terribly, which was what he wanted me to do, to clean myself out." Then, she remembers, while the film grew, Reisz "had to tell me an awful lot of things—technical things and things about acting."[16]

That she indeed learned a great deal about film acting from Reisz is especially evident during the love scenes. In them she is very successful in using her face and body with such effective subtlety as to make us truly believe that her character could love the man, even if he is so exasperating. At other times, however, her performance is slightly mannered, and thus lacking in a certain amount of conviction. Because of that, an unusual thing often happens in the movie. When the two characters are on the screen at the same time, but not making love, despite Redgrave's great beauty and presence, it is David Warner off whom we can't take our eyes.

David Warner's Performance

What is it about Warner that is so fascinating? Simply put, like Albert Finney in the role of Arthur Seaton, he is nothing less than perfect in playing Morgan. We believe in him so thoroughly that he dominates our complete attention.

Casting him in the lead role must not have been an automatic thing, however. It was, after all, going to be his first major role in a film. Besides, he hardly looked the part of a matinee idol. Yet it is easy to imagine that it was precisely his strange appearance which first caught Reisz's attention. In any event, casting him in the lead role was an extremely fortunate decision. Even the critics, who find so much to disagree about in *Morgan!*, are almost unanimous in their praise for Warner. And it is usually very high praise. David Paletz, for instance, thinks that his "slow and inexorable transition from gorilla fantasy to reality is a minor gem of movement, voice, increasingly reproachful eyes, and olfactory gestures. And even when ensconced in gorilla outfit he remains human."[17] And Alex Walker, not known for effusiveness, writes that what "works dazzingly well" in *Morgan!* is Warner's "incarnation of the Divine Fool. His bizarre physique could not be bettered. Gaunt, angular, flint-eyed and feral, he generates the dumb, wounded strength of wild animals which makes people sponsor protection societies. At times he looks like a Saxon warrior who has landed in the modern world through some confusing timeslip; elsewhere he seems to date from an even earlier eon of history and he does not really need to pull on his gorilla suit to convince us that he prefers the fantasy company of the tree-tops to the humans at ground level. Warner generates a prehensile nimbleness, a brute gentleness, an age-old jungleness, and gives one of the most bizarre and brilliant performances in the 1960s cinema."[18] High praise, indeed, but with which it is easy to be in complete agreement.

As for the supporting cast, its members are invariably very good. Robert Stephens as Napier exhibits just the right combination of bemusement and ire which his part calls for. Nan Munro as Leonie's mother is particularly good when she is asked to change from a state of shock to one of fury after she accidentally sets off Morgan's small bomb. In the role of Wally the Gorilla, Arthur Mullard couldn't be better. He looks just right, first of all, because of his wrestler's body and his bony, coarse-featured head. And, if gorillas could talk, their English might sound like his—slightly slurred, whining, and guttural. In the role of Morgan's mother Irene Handl is also very fine, especially in her ability to slaughter the English language. She stretches, flattens, twists, and wrenches it with no show of mercy. It's a marvelous parody of what agonies some people make their language go through. Thus in the film, next to the character of Morgan, the English language seems to suffer the most.

In conclusion, then, despite some flaws *Morgan!* is one of Reisz's richest and best films. It is also one of the finest examples of the British cinema coming out of the 1960s, a period when movies of high spirit and adventurous technique made one think immediately of the British influence.

5

Isadora

IN HIS NEXT FILM, coming out about two years after *Morgan!*, Reisz focuses on yet another character risking destruction by daring to be radically different. In this case, however, the subject is an actual figure from recent history, Isadora Duncan. Today the general public might know little, if anything, about her. But, as Louis Untermeyer has pointed out, early in this century a "one-woman revolution in the dance" which started in Europe and spread across the world was brought about by this "reckless but resolute young American . . . ."[1] What is more, he added, this woman "brought about a revolution not only in the dance but in the modern mind, healthier for her pioneering art. Actress as well as artist, she essayed many roles and overplayed them all—the delayed adolescent, the disillusioned femme fatale, the discursive Chorus, the Tragic Queen."[2] Obviously, Isadora's life story offers a promising subject for a film biography. Yet this kind of movie carries a built-in problem which too often has not been solved. Countless movies have been made about exciting, revolutionary figures of the past. Most of those have been dreary disappointments. Why? It seems that it all comes down to a question of attitude. How is one to deal with someone who is considered to be an immortal, especially if that person is a divinity of great art? Too many filmmakers have thus far responded with one of two extremes—they have treated their figures as "just people" who happen to have sublime talents, or as revered beings who have risen above mere mortality because of their talents. Reisz chose to avoid either extreme. Instead he strove to recreate and interpret the humanity as well as the greatness of Isadora, her absurdities and her beauty, her contradictions and her complexities.

85

Vanessa Redgrave as dancer Isadora Duncan enjoys the plaudits of a Russian crowd

In other words, he tried to be true to the paradoxical nature which can be found to reside in any great human being. This critical attitude, existing in a creative tension with a measure of romantic enthusiasm, is ultimately responsible for a splendid, even if imperfect, film biography.

The pity is that *Isadora* might deserve even higher praise if the entire film that Reisz had in mind were at hand. Unfortunately, today only a shrunken version is left. When the film was first shown, it was about three hours long. Because some officials at Universal decided that this was too long for a movie if it were going to be a commercial success, almost fifty minutes were finally cut from it with Reisz's "unwilling help."[3] Naturally, much of what was valuable was lost. Estelle Changas, a critic who saw the original version and thus could compare it with the present form, claims that, worst of all, much of the "impact of the rich and startling contrast between past and present" is now lost since "most of the scenes dealing with the aging Isadora have been cut." Moreover, she recalls, the performance of Vanessa Redgrave "suffers, too, from the loss of many interesting details which she established in her depiction of the aging Dancer."[4] Hence it is a wonder that the film wasn't totally mutilated by the massive cutting.

Structure

That *Isadora* was saved from disaster was in large part due to the fact that Reisz himself was involved in recutting the film. Because of his great talent for editing, he managed to perform wonders with the film he still had left to work with. Most important, he managed to retain a structure which made eminent sense. The film begins with a prologue which shows the twelve-year-old Isadora swearing her dedication to beauty and truth and sealing that vow by burning her parents' marriage certificate as if it were a ritualistic sacrifice. Then, following the credits, the film jumps forward to Isadora dictating her memoirs. It is now 1927, and because her inclusive years of life were indicated in the prologue, we know that it is the year of her death. This note of fatalism now becomes a dominant one, largely because of the purposely fragmented structure which follows.

Reisz now begins to cut from the present back to the past and back to the present again, until the film ends with Isadora's death. Moreover, at certain points he intercuts some of Isadora's personal fantasies and visions. This fragmented, incidental structure allows us to learn about Isadora gradually, in bits and pieces, as we might get to know someone in real life. Also, because the structure has some resemblance to the flux of memory, the impression is at times created that we are in the mind of Isadora. This feeling of intimacy is especially powerful during Isadora's death visions. Then we are forced to imagine her anguish with such intensity that it is like a personal experience of dread. This feeling of dread becomes increasingly powerful in the film—so that eventually each time the film cuts from the past to the present, or from the present to Isadora's vision of the death of her children, it is like a leap from life to impending doom. When the movie ends, it is with a stunning scene of Isadora's death. If we have responded to the structure of the story with sympathetic imagination, this is what we must fear and expect.

The film's structure is meant to disturb the reader in another way, too. It is going to disorient any audience naive enough to expect a story with a clear, simple line. Obviously, this is something which Reisz had in mind as part of his thematic strategy. Life, he might say, isn't neat like a well-made novel. Instead, it is more often very haphazard. Yet, because it wouldn't do to make a chaotic, confused movie about the chaos of life, Reisz is extremely careful to link the various scenes in his picture with very imaginative transitions. These links, sometimes quite subtle, are largely responsible for the satisfying feeling that a true work of art has been formed out of Isadora's tumultuous story.

Transitional Devices

These transitional devices take various forms and sometimes have more than one function. Only rarely does Reisz use a transitional link in a conventional way. When he does, however, they are totally appropriate. When he uses fade-outs, for instance, they are meant to imply the end of an important scene, the end of an important phase in Isadora's life, or the passage of time.

When Reisz uses cuts, on the other hand, he uses them in such a way as not only to relate the different scenes but also to make a personal, usually ironic, comment. There are many examples of this, but several are especially effective because they can surprise us with their imagination.

One especially good example of verbal transition occurs early in the film. After Isadora's first professional dancing performance in the movie, she is coaxed by the man who hired her to think about amplifying her act. Since he is talking about her continuing to perform in a beer palace in Chicago while she has dreams of conquering Europe, she isn't interested in his proposal. As Isadora tells him, she is going to leave because she is after her "destiny." The film then cuts to the present, the year of Isadora's death. She is now seen listening to the song "Bye, Bye, Blackbird," which turns out to be a highly ominous tune in the rest of the movie. Then she sees a young man clad in black, wearing a white tie. As it happens, he eventually turns out to be an agent of her fearful destiny. Thus the word "destiny," acting like a subtle echo, forms a link with sinister connotations.

There are other verbal bridges which depend on playful illusions. In one scene Isadora is telling a young admirer that she adores lions. Immediately the film gives way to a flashback which begins with the dramatic entrance of a caped figure into a hall where Isadora is practicing. It is Gordon Craig, Isadora's first lover in the film, and certainly a lion in a number of ways. In a later scene, another lover, Paris Singer, promises a bored Isadora that he will get her a beautiful young pianist as an accompanist to her dancing. The film then cuts to a long, high angle shot of someone making an entrance in a cape. It isn't a "lion" this time, though. It's a "frog." That is, Singer, inspired by latent jealousy, has hired a pianist who is at first physically abhorent to Isadora since he looks like a frog to her. Needless to say, the joke later turns on Singer, for eventually the pianist is transformed into something beautiful in Isadora's mind. To her he becomes a "frog prince," and another of her lovers.

Several of the most cunning transitions work through the junction of sexual comments and images. One such example takes place as the love interlude between Isadora and Craig is approaching its end. In a touchingly romantic scene the lovers are first seen lying together on the floor before a burning stove, with Isadora wondering out loud whether it was possible to die of love. Quickly, the picture cuts to a very pregnant Isadora, shot in profile, running toward the surf of some remote beach. It is, of course, significant that not long thereafter Isadora will think that she just might die from the fruits of love. For she will scream and scream with her birth pains, and Craig will be somewhere halfway around the world. It is also significant that in the rest of the movie love and death will be continuously yoked together by the sea.

In a lighter vein, Reisz uses this kind of ironically suggestive transition to stress the fact that Isadora was indeed a very sexy woman. Thus after Isadora decides that she might be interested in Singer as a lover, she encourages him to be less formal with her, to call her simply by her first name. The very next thing we see is Isadora waking up in Singer's enormous bed. What better way to say that they wasted no time getting there after the formalities were dropped? Because Singer is obviously grateful for Isadora's unhesitating response, he is soon offering her a key to the dancing school he has bought her. Immensely pleased, she replies by telling him that she wished to have *all* of her children by such beautiful men as Singer. Immediately thereafter, we see dozens of children, all dancing around a pregnant Isadora. It's as if not only her artistic dream but also her sexual one have come true.

The most poignant example of Reisz's use of ironic verbal linkage is found late in the film. After a provocative performance in Boston which causes a riot and empties the house, Isadora stands alone on the stage and cries out, "Don't let them tame you!" This is followed by a picture of an older, sadder, and tamer Isadora standing in another kind of emptiness. She is in the process of selling her possessions, and thus she is clinging for the last time to the draperies which represent her greater past.

Several of Reisz's most revealing cuts, however, use nonverbal sound as transitional devices. Of the various such examples, one clearly stands out. Late in the film Isadora performs before a large gathering of Russian soldiers. The performance, after it is interrupted by the failure of the electricity, ends in triumph. It ends with Isadora exciting some of the soldiers to the point where they join her in dancing on the stage, with the whole audience finally chanting her name in an ecstasy of approval. Then the film jumps forward to Isadora's last days. The first thing we now see is a shot pointed down on the water of the Mediterranean, while the sound of the chant overlaps and then dies out. Because the sea by now has become an ominous image in the movie, and because the dying chant suggests the fading glory of Isadora, the colliding scenes of past and present merge to create an exceedingly mournful impression.

Of course, a number of the most lively moments in the film are created through transitional sound effects, too. One particularly good example occurs during the birth of Isadora's first child. At the beginning of the scene Isadora is pictured repeatedly screaming from the pains of labor. As the camera points down on her while yet another of her terrified screams builds up, there is a sudden cut to a close-up of a baby screaming as it is brought into the world. Then, as the child is lifted up, a beaming Isadora is discovered behind it. It's a very clever way of stressing the related pains and joys which motherhood was destined to mean to Isadora.

There are a number of other transitional cuts where verbal or nonverbal sounds have such clever functions. But the wittiest cut of all in the movie is primarily visual. It follows the most enchanting scene in the story. The setting is Craig's loft at night. The shadows are deep except for the places where the bright moonlight falls. While Craig is trying to paint the light where it is streaming through a window, Isadora prances about naked, calling on the moon to hold still for her lover so that he can capture its magic forever, then playfully expressing her defiance of it when Craig suggests that the moon responds only to virgins. The very next shot is wonderfully ironic. It pictures Isadora in daylight sitting in front of a stove, her feet in a basin of hot water, suffering from a heavy cold. It's as if she has suddenly been yanked from a dream world into the perfectly mundane. We are bound to react with a smile, but also with a measure of sympathetic regret. What a pity that, in the words of one critic, such "romantic souls are forever being put upon by reality."[5]

One final thing needs to be said about Reisz's choice of transitions in his reedited version of *Isadora*. Obviously, the film exhibits a keen sense of structure throughout. But its pacing seems to flag somewhat as it moves toward the end. This is partly due to a shift in tone which is built into the film. Isadora's story is presented in a rather lighthearted, even mischievous way at first. As she grows older, however, and especially after the death of her children begins to haunt her, the tone becomes ever more melancholy. Reisz stresses this shift by using an editing strategy which becomes less and less witty and sardonic. As a result, one of two things happens to the viewer, probably depending on how conscious he is of film stylistics. His interest may begin to languish because the story becomes increasingly less lively or lighthearted. Or he may feel that, through this means, Reisz is purposely creating an increasing sense of anxiety about the thrust of the film—toward disaster.

Key Scenes

The built-in anxiety can be discovered in yet another significant way, by analyzing the key scenes in *Isadora*. The first scene to come after the credits begins deceptively. There is a lovely picture of the blue sea, the frame bordered by the green of verdure and the air full of the sounds of birds and the waves. Then the camera begins to dolly back, and suddenly a veil seems to appear before it. As the camera continues to move back, we see that it is actually Isadora's scarf, one end bound around her head, the other held out with her hand. Already Reisz has introduced three ominous motifs into the picture—the sea, the song of the birds, and the scarf. In the rest of the movie they will play important roles in her tragedy.

After the initial sounds of the birds and the sea, we begin to hear Isadora dictating her memoirs. "My first idea of movement of the dance," she begins, "came from the rhythm of the waves. And my first understanding of music from the sighing of the winds in the giant redwoods. For I was born by the sea, and all the great events of my life have taken place by a sea. I was born under the star of Aphrodite, goddess of love." As she says later, she doesn't have the natural eloquence of a Sir Walter Scott. But what she has said thus far is certainly expressive of her elemental vision of life. Moreover, some of these dictated thoughts gain in ironic resonance as the scene continues.

The next thing we hear is the playing of "Bye, Bye, Blackbird." While the song goes on, the camera continues to pull back, and then Isadora begins to join in the song. Now inside the room, the camera shows us a young man at a desk putting down Isadora's dictation on a typewriter. The *mise-en-scène* takes on symbolic implications, for as Isadora enters the room, the camera follows her while she glides around the desk which sits in the middle, giving us glimpses of the hopeless clutter of the room, significant, by implication, of Isadora's cluttered life in general. The scene ends with Isadora reclining and saying, "I'm only a poor dancer, and all

I know about is dancing." This self-effacing statement is an effective
way to end the scene because it has an important double edge.
First, it is an early sign in the movie that Isadora will look upon
her past in a parodic way. Second, it becomes apparent that perhaps
after all Isadora really understood only dancing.

Hence in this introductory scene, appropriately shot in one continuous take, Reisz has in a way created a microcosm of Isadora's
experiential world. It begins with natural beauty, is followed by
signs of misfortune, and ends with a touch of ironic self-recognition.

Of course, the theme of misfortune, or outright disaster, is expressed with the most wrenching force in those later scenes where
Isadora has visions of the death of her two children. The first such
vision takes place while Isadora and Mary, her faithful companion
during her last years, are in a car on their way to Paris. It is a
strikingly brilliant day, just the kind to make one forget the problems
of life. Then the car approaches a tunnel, and Isadora's blithe mood
is shattered.

The camera zooms toward the tunnel, as if racing toward a self-
destructive collision, and a painfully high-pitched sound begins to
build. Through this technique, Reisz has suddenly forced us to
identify with Isadora's state of mind. From this subjective perspective, the angle of vision shifts to a dramatic close-up of Isadora's
face as the tunnel's darkness falls over it. A moment of silence
follows, and at the same time we see the faces of two children,
pressed against the back window of a car, pulling away. Then we
see Isadora's face again in close-up, and we hear the sound of her
moaning cry mixed with the rushing wind and the roaring echo of
the car. This confusion of sounds, effectively expressing her state
of panic, stops when the car finally emerges into the light. But the
look of terror remains on Isadora's face, because she has just been
reminded of the greatest tragedy in her life, the loss of her two
children by drowning.

Later in the film the full torment of this loss is expressed in a
long scene which has an agonizing effect. It begins when Isadora,
while playing with a deck of Tarot cards, turns up a combination
which means death by water. As soon as she discovers this, she
turns to look directly at the camera, her head to the left of the
center of the screen, as if to make us aware that what is to follow
is most intimate and unsettling.

Again we hear the piercing sound which began the vision in the tunnel, now functioning like a refrain of Isadora's apprehension. Immediately thereafter a shot down on the water follows, the image suffused with light. The camera pans to the right, and we see horses and men struggling to pull a car out of the water. This is the children's death car, and yet the scene is extremely picturesque.

The explanation for this apparent paradox can be found in the mind of Isadora, who is next seen writing and thinking out loud about the death of her children. In her mind, the vision is both appalling and beautiful, a mixture of death and art. To emphasize this confusion, the shot began with a blurred image of Isadora.

After the shot comes into sharp focus, the camera begins to pull back slowly. Then as Isadora is recalling the premonitions she had of the death of her children, the camera begins to move back toward her. All at once we see the image of the children looking through the car window again. As the car pulls away, Isadora waves goodbye. A cut follows to a close-up of her, and then the camera begins to pull back once more, as if it wishes to be intimate with Isadora's tragedy yet is hesitant about intruding on her personal agony.

As this sequence continues, it becomes even more rhythmic. Also, Isadora's death vision becomes more and more subjective. For example, it is *her* cry we hear when we see the car plunge off a bridge into the river below, and it is a black mourning dress she seems to be wearing *before* the children leave in the death car. Moreover, the vision grows ever more beautiful, until finally we see a stunningly gorgeous shot. In it the top of the death car is first seen floating on the Seine, and then the camera begins to pull back farther and farther, until the picture resembles a lovely impressionistic canvas that might have been painted by Renoir. In Isadora's mind, it seems, her tragedy has truly been transformed into a work of art.

After that dazzling shot, there is a cut to an extreme close-up of Isadora still going through torture at her writing desk. The camera once again begins to pull back, and then returns, while she tries to understand the true meaning of her agony. What she now concludes is that she was destined to be pursued by personal tragedy. What we understand is that, after the death of her children, she tended to look upon life with the imagination of disaster.

The last scene of the film summarizes the fatalism of Isadora's story perfectly. Like the scene which comes right after the prologue, it begins with a beautiful view of the Mediterranean, except that

it is much more romantic. At first we hear the overlapping of Isadora's voice singing about love, then the strains of a tango while
the camera moves toward a dancing pier jutting into the sea.

A cut to the dancing area follows. Into the frame walks Bugatti,
a man whom Isadora has been looking for. By now he has become
a clearly sinister figure, suggestive of the fate which Isadora is
pursuing and which is also pursuing her. Consequently, what Reisz
does next is ideal in stylistic terms. He begins to circle the camera,
from Bugatti, around the dancing floor, and, completing the circle,
to the entrance of Isadora. The circle, which at first appears to be
simply a functional strategy, is highly symbolic, of course. Above
all, it stresses the inevitable connection between Isadora, dancing,
and her unhappy fate.

When Isadora arrives at the dancing area she is blindfolded by
some of her admiring friends. This suggestion of unresisting blind-
ness is emphasized even more by the fact that the scarf which is
tied around her eyes is the same one which we have repeatedly
seen in the film. It is the one Isadora has been wearing all along
since she started her search for Bugatti. She will wear it when she
dies. In fact, it will be the means of her death.

After the blindfold is taken off, she sways gracefully toward Bugatti, as if spellbound. When they begin to dance to the tango which
is still playing, they make a striking couple. She is dressed in firy
red, he in black with a white tie, the colors pointedly symbolic of
desire and death.

As they continue their dance, it becomes more elegant and more
electrifying. By the time they finish, they have aroused all of the
other dancers. There is a burst of applause and cheering when they
end their performance. It is another "triumph" for Isadora—but
only in an ironic way. At the end of the dance she kneels to Bugatti
as if in submission, foreshadowing her imminent fate.

Once the tango number is over, the next one should by this time
be expected. Naturally, it's "Bye, Bye, Blackbird," the first song
we heard Isadora sing, and now the last song which we will hear
in the movie. The implied analogy between Bugatti and the blackbird imagery of the song is, of course, established by this time.
Death and fate are the links. Thus when Isadora and Bugatti next
whirl about to the first notes of this number, it's another foreshadowing of her death.

Isadora's end comes quickly thereafter. As she and Bugatti race off in the car, and she stands up in her excitement, her scarf flows back. With brutal suddenness, it catches in a back wheel, twists around it and her neck, and kills her.

After flashing a shocking close-up of her gaping face, Reisz does some things which are meant to broaden the meaning of Isadora's fate. After Bugatti leans over her, and then leaves, the camera is used very expressively. It moves back slightly, then slowly forward. Significantly, this means moving at first directly toward the dancing area which Isadora and Bugatti have just left. What is consequently seen is what Isadora has literally and symbolically left behind—a younger generation dancing to "Bye, Bye, Blackbird." Then, as the camera continues to move forward, it passes over the dancers and comes to rest on the sea. This is, of course, appropriate for a story about Isadora. Yet is is appropriate in a more general way, too.

The final shot down on the sea holds for a very long time, with "Bye, Bye, Blackbird" heard clearly at first, then fading into silence, followed by the barely audible sound of the splash of waves. Finally, the color turns to black and white, then to black as we read "The End." By this ending Reisz evidently wishes to stress two things about Isadora—that her revolution seemed to end in personal futility, and that indeed all existence does. Such an interpretation appears unavoidable when one dwells on the final contrasting imagery—between the beautiful, romantic setting of the dancing pier and the horror of Isadora's strangled face; between the elegant dancing of Isadora and the jerky, jazzy movements of the other dancers; and between the message of "Bye, Bye, Blackbird" and the final sounds of the dark sea.

Irony

If the film verges on outright despair or cynicism, it doesn't cross the line. What saves it is, not surprisingly, Reisz's sense of irony. In this film, as indeed in all of his feature films thus far, that is a persistent tone. Consequently, the impression is left that Reisz believes, given life as it is, the only proper or possible response for an intelligent man is one of irony. It is like a form of creative, personal salvation. With an ironic vision, life can become more tolerable, even beautiful, and certainly more interesting.

We have already seen that this attitude charges the basic structure of *Isadora*. What remains is to see it function in the movie in still other important and provocative ways.

Reisz's use of color, for instance, is very shrewd even though *Isadora* is his first full-length feature in color. Certainly much of the credit should go to Jocelyn Herbert when it comes to the design of the several grand set pieces. There are some pointed color choices, however, which clearly have the mark of Reisz's style. The colors of Isadora's dancing garments, for example, invariably have a carefully planned value. Naturally, she wears white when in the purest state, especially when she is young and innocent. In addition, she wears white when she is pregnant and very happy while teaching the children at the dancing school which Singer bought for her. She also happens to be in white while she dances to the music of the pianist whom Singer hired for her, but with a yellow scarf added, a sign of the approaching infidelity. When at one point she performs to the impassioned music of Beethoven, she is wearing purple. Mostly, though, she appears in vivid red. Eventually this color assumes more than one meaning: revolutionary fervor and self-destruction, for instance. But when Singer is observed first watching Isadora perform on stage, the meaning is purely sexual.

What we initially see then is what appears to be an iris shot of Isadora, clad in a diaphanous red garment, moving very sensually. When the point of view shifts to a shot of Singer looking at her through his opera glasses, we connect the iris image with the glasses. Naturally, we can also now imagine why Singer was so aroused by Isadora. The circular image is extremely erotic, even aggressive, in a Freudian sense.

Isadora desires a measure of sexual aggression from her men. Ironically, Singer isn't all that he initially appears to be. At the start of their affair, Isadora wonders if he isn't like Zeus assuming various shapes and forms by which he might ravage a woman. She imagines him as a bull, for instance. In truth, however, he turns out to be more like the stuffed tiger and peacock which are found in his enormous English home.

As for the other men who play a prominent role in Isadora's life, she initially thinks of them in terms of aggressive animals, too. They, however, also fail to live up to her early impressions. Essenin, the Russian poet who comes along after she is forty years old, turns out to be more of a petulant child than the tiger she seemed to think she was getting. Craig, on the other hand, seemed for a while to be a kind of lion. But when he and Isadora part, he is more like the piece of driftwood which he carries during their last scene together.

This parting scene, by the way, is a very effective one because of the acute ironic contrast which exists between what is said and what we see. Isadora and Craig chatter happily, mainly about the future. Yet all the time the *mise-en-scène* belies their romantic optimism. Shot mostly in long shot and deep focus, the scene shows them against an immensely cold, empty backdrop. Naturally, because it's an important part of Isadora's story, this "great event" takes place by the sea. On this occasion, the sea is appropriately choppy and gray. The beach is barren of life and color. When Isadora and Craig have their parting kiss, they are photographed in extreme long shot. Then the two small figures separate, and the distance between them stretches into a long line from the left upper corner of the frame down to the right. Emphasizing the finality of their parting even more, when Craig turns and walks off alone he disappears over the crest of a dune, as if swept away.

By contrast, it was Isadora who was suddenly carried away when she first met Craig. That is, he carried her away to his place in a coach, and soon thereafter he seduced her. Significantly, though, she was seduced less by his charm and spirit than by her own artistic imagination. This is illustrated by Reisz in a brilliant fashion, as Estelle Changas points out so well in her analysis of the scene: "The episode with Craig, her first lover, an artist as ethereal and egocentric as Isadora, dramatizes the way in which Isadora utilizes the raw experiences of life, transforming reality into the form and rhythm of the dance. As the two make love in Craig's barren studio, Isadora fantasizes in a flash-forward, envisioning herself alone, performing a new dance which epitomizes her fulfillment (dancing to Isadora is primarily the expression of her sexuality), and is more dramatically erotic than the couple's physical passion. Ironically, the love-making excites her creativity (quite a departure from the typical feminine blackout depicted during sexual intercourse), as the cross-cutting makes clear. In her most intimate moments Isadora sees herself as more artist than woman. Appropriately, Craig seduces her through the language of art—she cannot resist the vision he has of her as a revolutionary, a priestess. When Craig disrobes her and pronounces her body magnificent, he makes an aesthetic evaluation, not a sexual response. And her unabashed affirmation of her own beauty is equally comic because it is unfeminine. It is artistic vanity, pride in the instrument of one's art."[6]

Estelle Changas has been quoted again, and at length this time, because her review of *Isadora* is, unfortunately, so exceptional in its serious analysis of Resiz's intent. Too many of the critics who have reviewed the film manage to focus mainly just on plot and acting. Too little is ever ventured about Reisz's stylistics or artistic vision. Thus most of the reviews of *Isadora* are only too predictable and shallow. Those which find fault with the movie tend to dwell on what they see as the inevitable choppiness resulting from the forced reediting. Having made this convenient point, it seems as if they don't feel an obligation to really think about the extent of the validity of their conclusion. Those who praise the film (and, as it happens, most reviews do) tend to focus at length only on the performance of Vanessa Redgrave in the role of Isadora.

Vanessa Redgrave's Performance

This acting performance, to be sure, deserves any amount of praise. Vanessa Redgrave is simply smashing. She provides the film with a magnetic force which is always exciting and gives shape to the whole work. And this is true even if a great deal of her most sensitive acting was cut out of the version which was finally exhibited.

After what she recalled as the highly rewarding experience of *Morgan!*, she was naturally happy to work with Reisz again. But that only begins to explain her passionate involvement in the story of Isadora. It has become evident in recent years that her identification with the dancer was actually quite personal, at least on the subconscious level. It seems that she really believed in most of the revolutionary principles that Isadora stood for. As a result, it was a kind of dream role for her in a political sense. Of course, it was a dream role in an artistic way, too. Here was an acting role which demanded not only introspective discipline but also elaborate versatility—just the kind of role which Reisz himself loves to develop.

One of the most demanding things she had to do was to play Isadora from the age when she was starting in the dancing business to her death. This she managed to do so well that, even in the truncated version, one is made to feel intensely the various phases which an artist, and a woman, may have to go through.

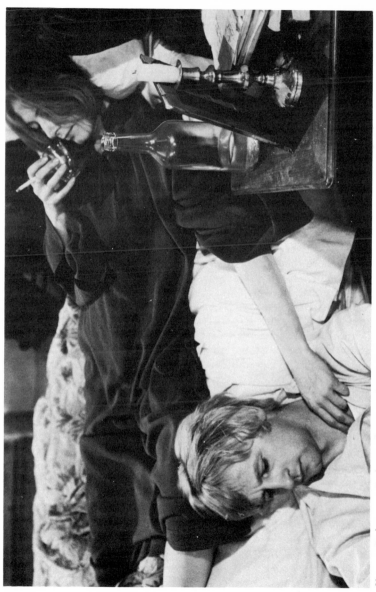

Venessa Redgrave as Isadora with Ivan Tchenko as her Russian lover, soon to become her husband

She is particularly impressive as Isadora in her last year. With the finest touch, she creates a character who is bold and frightened, absurd and gay, eager for more life yet sliding into self-pity and irrationality. To get this complex effect, she uses a number of interesting techniques. Sometimes she smacks her lips and gestures with her hands with the exaggeration of a dowager. At other times she is a phantom of the young dancer, moving with painful grace. Her hair is slightly garish and her face is marked with the splotches resulting from heavy drinking, but the swollen eyes can still express an ardent vision of life. As for her voice, what Vanessa Redgrave does with it is truly amazing.

It's not just that she apes the American dialect almost to perfection. The range of her nimble voice reveals as much as anything the complex character of Isadora. In scene after scene it rises or falls or turns to express the true emotions of the dancer. Particularly in those scenes where she is dictating her memoirs, the voice tells much more than meets the eye. If one listens carefully, there is on occasion a self-mocking element. It is there to reveal Isadora's recognition that, in some ways, she has become a parody of her former greatness. In the chronological context of the story, Vanessa Redgrave's voice seems to actually grow older, coarser, like Isadora. Thus it ranges from the sweet laughter of her youth, for example, to the sporadic harsh outbursts of her final wayward year.

Finally, Vanessa Redgrave's dancing is deserving of praise as well. She is not a particularly gifted dancer, as it happens. However, with the help of Litz Pisk, the choreographer, she managed to use her body to the fullest advantage. Thus, for instance, in one performance where she is dancing to a Sousa march in the Chicago beer palace, we can fully imagine the excitement which brings the crowd to its feet as she boldly kicks high with her long legs. During her performances to classical pieces, on the other hand, she is especially adept at interpreting the music for us with her graceful arms and long, expressive fingers. In each case, as one dance critic has pointed out, she "has sought not to dance *like* Isadora, but to allow Isadora's precepts to permeate her own quite different body."[7] Because she succeeds in this so well, her dancing at times has the real illusion of greatness.

The best such example is her performance of Beethoven's Seventh Symphony, the work which, appropriately enough, was called the apotheosis of the dance by no less a person than Wagner himself.

Aided by a gracefully mobile camera, Vanessa Redgrave creates an experience which is full of enchantment. The most magical moment comes when she dances around and around the stage and the turning camera which follows her. The look on her face is pure rapture, and her swaying body and hands express a world of beautiful desire.

Flaws in the Film

Unfortunately, Reisz isn't so well served by all of his performers in this movie. James Fox in the role of Craig is the most effective member of the supporting cast. He projects just the right kind of wry, relaxed self-importance which could attract the young Isadora. Most of the rest of a very large cast are at least competent. But in two of the major supporting roles the film suffers to some extent. One is the role of the Russian poet. Ivan Tchenko somehow fails to project intensely enough that sense of unstable rage, of confused genius, which the story called for. The other role is that of Singer. Surprisingly enough, Jason Robards's interpretation of him constitutes an obvious flaw in the film.

The problem is that his performance is so very dull and stiff. It is true that Singer himself is supposed to be a rather insipid person. This is clearly written into the script, for he has the film's most inane, tedious lines. Moreover, one of the intents of the movie is to suggest character through background imagery. Therefore Singer's dullness is emphasized, for example, through the use of plain colors, the cold texture of marble and statuary, and the previously mentioned dead-animal imagery. Robards's mannered performance of a bore is thus a form of overkill. Better if he had played the dullard with less technique and more imagination or suppressed wit.

Because of Robards's stiff performance, the section of the movie where Isadora is living with Singer sometimes tends to drag a bit. Another part of the film, however, seems almost interminable. It is a scene where Isadora dances before a gathering of Russian soldiers, and it is the one part of the film which is stylistically flawed. It is meant to be one of the most significant scenes, for it is supposed to show in a condensed way what Isadora's experience in Russia was like—how she was an inspirational guiding light to both adults and children during a very bad time. There is some extremely effective use of cross-editing which links the experience of the young and the old who came in contact with Isadora. Nevertheless, by and large, the scene fails, partly because the camera seems too anxious, too nervous on occasion. The unfortunate result is that, at certain points, it becomes obvious what has been planned, why the camera has to move this way and that. Moreover, the scene fails because it is so very sentimental. As the scene goes on and on, it seems less and less genuine. At the end one must suspect that it was staged and performed without Reisz's full conviction, or even attention.

If the movie has any other imperfections, however, they are so minor that it would be quibbling to dwell on them. Because, all in all, even in its shortened version, *Isadora* is simply one of the best film biographies ever made.[8]

6

The Gambler

IT WAS 1974 before Reisz's next picture, *The Gambler*, came out. Why the long period of six years between films? There were several reasons, and the first one had to do with the final fate of *Isadora*. Reisz may have put up a stoical front, but underneath he was deeply hurt by the severe cutting which his movie was forced to undergo. Consequently, for about a year after *Isadora* appeared in its shortened form, he recalls that he existed in a kind of inertia while "licking my wounds."[1]

After that he threw himself with restored will into a new project. This was an ambitious adaptation of *The Naive and Sentimental Lover*, a novel by John Le Carré. For a period of time, he now recalls, he worked with great vigor. Then, however, it became increasingly clear that this undertaking was going to go nowhere. Somehow, despite every effort, it seemed that Reisz and his collaborators would never be quite able to transfer the excitement which existed in the novel to a scenario. Thus the project was finally abandoned.[2]

What followed was an even more ambitious undertaking. Carlo Ponti, having bought the rights to the famous novel, came to Reisz with the idea of turning André Malraux's *The Human Condition* (also called *Man's Fate*) into a film. This was exciting to Reisz, and he set eagerly to work. At first everything appeared to be going well. But this project was also destined to be aborted. This time the problem had little if anything to do with the art of filmmaking. Instead it was primarily a question of politics. The story, focusing on the 1927 Shanghai revolution, was meant to be realized with the support and involvement of China. At the beginning the Chinese

James Caan vignetted by a shadowy opponent in The Gambler

responded very favorably to the idea of the movie. They could evidently imagine some politically advantageous fall-out from such a film. But then the climate changed. Distrust, suspicion, skepticism, or even outright xenophobia appeared to set in. As a result, although Reisz wished passionately to finish this project, he had to abandon it, too.[3]

Then Reisz was asked to contribute to a series of adaptations of Chekhov stories which his friend Melvyn Bragg was producing for the television branch of the BBC. His response was to suggest *On the High Road*, a play which he had seen performed at an amateur theater several years earlier. Fortunately, this was one project which didn't fall through, and Reisz managed to finish it in time for a 1973 showing. But it would be yet another year before Reisz's next full-fledged movie would appear.

Reisz's involvement in making *The Gambler* began when the producers Robert Chartoff and Irwin Winkler approached him with the idea of making a film for them about gambling. This proposal was made, incidentally, without any clear assurance that it might not eventually fall through.[4] Yet Reisz accepted the offer, however tentative it might have been, not simply because he was anxious to make another film, but because he was drawn to the story which the screenplay he was given promised.

This screenplay was still in a very rough and undeveloped state, in truth little more than a documentary sketch about the world of gambling. Therefore, the first thing that Reisz did was to set to rewriting and amplifying it with its originator, James Toback. The two men reportedly began working together closely right after they first met. Nevertheless, it took many months, and by some accounts up to two years, to actually finish the script.[5] Reisz, of course, prefers to work slowly and carefully. In this case, however, the reason why the process of completing the screenplay took so long was presumably because he and Toback found important matters to disagree about. Above all, they seemed to disagree, at least subconsciously, about how the central character ought to be perceived. That they never did completely resolve this issue is borne out by some unsatisfactory aspects which the finished picture has.

As far as the outline and structure of the story are concerned, there appears to have been no real problem. In its finished form, at least, the story moves in a direct, compelling line without any false steps. It starts by showing us the central character, Axel Freed, gambling in an underground establishment in New York, and losing heavily—in fact, to the tune of over $44,000. After this incredible run of bad luck, Axel must somehow come up with the money or face the very real danger of violence from the underworld characters to whom he owes the sum. He has limited means of his own, since he makes his living as an English teacher at a city college. Thus he is forced to find other means, and quickly. He sees a loan shark, but what he needs is too much for this particular crook. Then he goes to his mother, a doctor, who pulls out her savings for him.

He has the money now. Yet he can't resist flying off with his girl friend to Las Vegas for a quick trip to make more, so that he can pay back his mother as well as take care of the gambling debt, and so that he can again feel the ecstasy of winning. Before they fly off, however, he also bets on several basketball games because, as he tells a bookie, he feels "hot as a pistol." He wins in Las Vegas, big, but he also loses big on the bets he had made on the games. As a result, with time running out, he is worse off than ever before, since he has now even lost his mother's money. Consequently, to save himself, he is finally persuaded to try to corrupt a basketball player who attends his class into fixing a game.

After that game comes the final scene of the movie, taking place in that "underworld" known as Harlem, where Axel picks up a prostitute in a bar and goes with her to a sleazy hotel room. Once in the room, he seems to deliberately leave the door cracked open. Why he would want to do that soon becomes apparent. He has come to this room to take a final risk, to gamble with his life. This is why he gives the prostitute $50, only to take it back again. Naturally, she starts a row, and her pimp comes in. The pimp threatens Axel with a switch-blade knife pressed against his throat, but Axel just tells him to go ahead, that he is ready. When the pimp, confused, starts to turn away while guessing out loud that this white man must be crazy, Axel begins to beat him furiously, and then to kick him. The prostitute, screaming at Axel to stop it, finally picks up the knife which has fallen from the pimp's hand. As she strikes out with it, a flash freeze shows it slashing across Axel's cheek. Bleeding profusely, he now stumbles from the room, down the stairs, and into the seedy lobby of the hotel. There he stops in front of a mirror. As he looks at himself, or, more precisely, at his scar, a curious smile appears to form on his face. This is captured in a short freeze shot, and then, punctuated by cascading music, the film ends with a fade. It is a stunning last image. Yet it is ultimately unsatisfactory because it doesn't work successfully enough to resolve the final point of the movie.

Problems and Flaws

In this last scene we can make sense of Axel's motives in going "slumming" in Harlem in the first place. It seems obvious that in venturing there Axel is driven by the conflicting feelings of egoism fed by dangerous excitement and of self-disgust. He is, after all, on an emotional high after having survived the heavy odds against him once more, but he also knows that he has taken perhaps the final step toward self-degradation. Therefore, when the pimp threatens him with death, he takes the ultimate risk that he can win his life *and* he welcomes the possibility of his imminent, punitive death. But what are we then to make of what is written on his face in the final mirror image? This time, the possibilities are too many and too paradoxical to form a satisfying conclusion to the film. The "smile" on Axel's face can mean pain or joy, humility or pride, corruption or purgation, self-discovery or self-delusion. The list could actually go on, but the point has been made.

The ending, in short, is just the kind to make critics and other filmgoers disagree completely about what the movie is ultimately trying to say. Reisz, of course, invited serious discussion through the purposefully ambiguous endings which he invariably used in his earlier films. Obviously, he thought that it was one of the best ways to enrich a film's meaning and to increase its impact. And, to be sure, this strategy worked quite well for him in his previous work. However, in *The Gambler* the final image he chose is so ambivalent and even confusing that it constitutes an obvious flaw.

How did this happen with such a careful filmmaker as Reisz? It seems that for a logical explanation one has to go back to the apparent inability of Reisz and Toback to resolve some of their differences. The most prominent of these, signaled so clearly by the irresolution of the "smile," was their attitude toward Axel. Based on the occasional contradiction between script and style found in the rest of the film, Toback admired Axel to the point of identifying with him while Reisz had a detached, critical attitude toward him. To Reisz he seemed a type of character he has always been interested in, someone on the border between reason and madness, somewhat perverse, a victim of romantic folly.⁶ To Toback he seemed to be more of a heroic victim frustrated by the decadent modern world.

Toback's attitude is especially clear when Axel lectures to his students or when he makes a toast at his grandfather's eightieth birthday party. At those times one feels perhaps like Pauline Kael, who writes that the movie makes her feel as if she were "trapped at a maniacal lecture on gambling as existential expression."⁷

When Axel lectures his students on Dostoevsky's vision of life, we may be at first spellbound by the case he is presenting. Recalling that Dostoevsky, as a gambler, could say that sometimes two and two can make five, he tells the class that what this means, of course, is that the great man felt that life was based on will. In other words, he continues, Dostoevsky "claims an idea is true because he wants it to be true, because he says it is true. And the issue isn't whether he's right, but whether he has the will to believe he's right no matter how many proofs there are that say he's wrong." To conclude this argument, Axel quotes Dostoevsky himself: "Reason only satisfies man's rational requirements. Desire, on the other hand, encompasses everything. Desire is life." Axel's argument is so carefully worked out, and is delivered with such conviction, that we are bound to be impressed with Dostoevsky's thinking at first. Then we quickly begin to see that he is talking as much about himself as about the Russian writer. This would be all well and good if the connection were made with more subtlety and if the lecture's real aim, to educate us, were not made to look so obvious. Apparently we aren't, however, trusted sufficiently to discover on our own what Axel believes in and what the theme of the film must stand for. Therefore we are told, in so many words, that we should live like Dostoevsky by taking risks and that we should consequently admire Axel's attempt to do so.

In a subsequent lecture to the same students on Washington, as if to hedge his bets, Toback's character is even more explicit about the importance of gambling. In brief, he comes to the conclusion, with William Carlos Williams, that Washington was a very disappointing character because he was so afraid of losing that he eliminated risk at any cost. Thus he had the primary American trait which D. H. Lawrence described in the following manner: "Americans fear new experience more than they fear anything. They are the world's greatest dodges because they dodge their own very

selves." Obviously, the theme of this lecture is that the father of
America and Americans in general are thoroughly disappointing
because they value security above everything else. True or not, the
problem with this and the previous lecture is that the movie seems
to come to a halt while we are told what to make of it.

This is even more obviously the case when Axel gives his eloquent
toast at his grandfather's birthday party. It is Axel's longest uninterrupted speech in the film, and it gives the clearest evidence of
what he values most in life. The toast begins with his pronounce-
ment that we are now "living in an age that subverts the breeding
of men" like his grandfather. A brief summary of the old man's life
then follows, a life led on the edge of chance, a violent and a heroic
life. This life, Axel says, has been a guide to him because it has
taught him to take risks, to dare. Then he ends by saying that he
lifts the toast to "this man that seized what he wanted with nothing
there to back him up but wit, and balls, and will. This killer, this
king." Although Axel gives the toast surrounded by a large group
of celebrants, it almost has the air of a soliloquy. Everything seems
to stop for the speech, and we are informed what is really in Axel's
mind, just how deep his yearning is to be a kind of "killer, king."
We also get the clear impression that whoever wrote the speech
(surely Toback) meant it as an inspiration for us all. But once it is
over, it becomes apparent that there is also an opposing view of
Axel's desire for a hazardous life at work in the film. To Reisz the
man seems more frenzied or deranged than just daring. Consequently at times the film has a kind of split vision which leads to
confusion.

There are some other, though certainly less serious, problems
with the film, and most of them have to do with the explicit nature
of the script, too. The film is much too literary, for instance. It is,
of course, entirely fitting for Axel to refer to Dostoevsky, Washington, and D. H. Lawrence in class. But must his bookie indicate
his admiration for Shakespeare so openly and must the grandfather
allude not only to Shakespeare but also to Whitman so freely? Then
there is a story told by Axel's girl friend about a cowboy named
Eugene. The trouble is that it parallels Axel's life too closely to have
any other function than as an obviously comparative case in point.
Also, because of its airtight quality, the script traps itself into dialogue which on occasion seems unnatural and forced.

One problem, however, which can't be blamed on the script is the casting of Lauren Hutton in the role of Axel's girl friend, Billie. Given her limited talent, Hutton simply isn't able to create the kind of character which is called for. What is required is for her to project someone caught between the attraction and the fear of Axel's fanaticism. However, in the words of one critic, she "may possess the face that launched a thousand lipsticks, but as an actress she remains monotonously monochromatic."[8]

Antonio Fargas in the supporting role of the Harlem pimp isn't very convincing, either. He overacts to the point of parody. But the rest of the large supporting cast is certainly very fine. Morris Carnovsky as the grandfather projects just the right hint of the charm which must have been lethal when he was a younger man. Jacqueline Brookes as the mother is especially effective in exhibiting her exasperation with and concern for her son. In addition, the supporting cast boasts a number of hoods and crooks played to perfection, without any simple condescension or melodramatics. Above all, there is Paul Sorvino as Axel's favorite bookie; but Carmine Caridi, Burt Young, and London Lee also stand out. There are still other supporting performances which might be praised. In fact, as is typical of Reisz's work, the acting in the film as a whole is clearly one of its outstanding features.

James Caan's Performance

This brings the discussion to James Caan in the role of Axel Freed. Guided by Reisz, he came up with what is no doubt his best performance to date. As a matter of fact, he was so good in the role that, largely because of him, the film does ultimately hold together better than might otherwise have been expected. Even if there are those critics who might not agree, it seems clear that he manages to project very convincingly that combination of complacency and quiet rage which suggests a madness on the flashpoint of explosion. It's the kind of acting job which must have been a test of stamina for Caan since, in the words of Pauline Kael, he was asked "to stay clenched, the bit in his teeth: an uncalculated move and the picture's tension would collapse."[9] Because Caan never loses his hold on his complex role, he does much to span the breach which exists between some aspects of the film's script and the style.

James Caan as Axel Freed in two tense moments in *The Gambler*: (top) showing his cool at the tables; (bottom) quarreling with his bookie, Jimmy, played by Carmine Caridi.

Film Style and Key Scenes

Reisz arrived at the style for *The Gambler* by basing it on what by this time had become something of an artistic formula in his anatomical films.[10] As he had done before, he begins with the central character and draws the shape, tone, and manner from him. This is why the shape of *The Gambler* resembles in certain ways that of an American suspense film. And this is also why its tone and manner are often ambiguous, pendent, and speculative. In addition, Reisz attempts to create a kind of double vision in this as in his previous work. That is, he purposely establishes a style in *The Gambler* which allows us to imagine the interior of the characters while encouraging us to retain at the same time an objective understanding of the surface truths. These interior and exterior angles of vision may tend, of course, to clash on certain occasions. But the resultant tensions, or even paradoxes, are kept from disrupting the film by means of yet another of Reisz's stylistic strategies. This is the use of a unified sensibility. That sensibility, also inspired by the central character, acts very much like the first-person point of view does in a novel, and thus contributes not only to a sense of organic unity but also to a feeling of inevitable continuity.

It bears emphasizing at this point that Reisz makes every effort to apply these as well as his other favored stylistics with the greatest possible subtlety. Hence they may be quite "invisible" to the casual viewer. If, however, a person is sufficiently concerned about how film style works, he can discover that Reisz's preferred dynamics are variously and persistently at work. And this is most obviously the case in the crucial scenes in one of his films, which coincidentally turn out to be almost always the most successful ones, too.

Certainly the first scene in *The Gambler* is one of these. It begins with a shot down on several cards being put down on the green gambling table which served as the backdrop for the credits. Then there follows a shot of Axel looking down, with tense concentration and anxiety, on what the table holds. After this, there are brief shots of his bookie warning him not to bet over the limit, and of Axel continuing to play and lose. This is all seen by way of a series of brief shots, so that one may begin to feel the tension which, bit by bit, is building up in Axel. Finally, having run up his losses to the breaking point, he walks out of the gambling place.

When he comes out of the building, his condition is reflected by the use of carefully expressive and subjective sound. There is first the highly oppressive theme music based on Mahler's First Symphony. It effectively suggests that feeling of dread which is beginning to envelop Axel. Then there follows an expressive use of "silence." As Axel comes out onto the street, traffic is seen to be whizzing back and forth between him and the camera. We at first hear the cars going by, but then we hear them less and less. Thus it's as if we are entering into Axel's state of mind, where there is no room for such incidentals as street noise. Only his desperate gambling situation is on his mind.

The next scene is equally effective because, after Axel gets into his car to drive off to work, Reisz uses some very successful flashback editing. Through these quick, rhythmic flashbacks we are allowed to see Axel recalling the disastrous night of losing game after game. Also we are allowed to see his bookie warn him in so many words that because of his enormous debt he is now in an extremely dangerous position. And through this means we can also clearly see that Axel is more disturbed than he would like to show. Thus, by using a purposely fragmenting technique, Reisz provides us with important plot and emotional information in an efficient and dramatic way.

Another very successful scene is where Axel wins his biggest game while he is on the quick trip to Las Vegas. It is introduced by a marvelous pan shot following a car in which we imagine Axel to be riding with his girl friend. Axel has been winning steadily at various tables, and now he and Billie are on their way to still another place. In the mind of Axel, a winning streak has the ecstatic quality of a sexual or religious experience. This is suggested by the pan shot. As it sweeps across, it picks up some fountains brightly lit in the shimmering night and rows of enchanting blue lights from hotels. It is a sensual, enthralling picture. And it provides just the right romantic, quasi-religious touch which can tell us how Axel might presently feel as it anticipates his upcoming moment of glory.

Glory is really not too big a word to use to describe what Axel will feel when he wins his next gamble. This gamble is one of those which proves, at least to him, what the power of will can do. He has eighteen showing on the table, and yet he asks for another card from the blackjack dealer, even doubling the bet as he does so. The dealer and Billie think he is crazy. But he *demands* the three, and he gets it.

To show just what Axel experiences during this moment, Reisz employs some brilliant stylistics. As Axel's instant of glory approaches, the slightly low camera eye begins to move in on him from a medium long distance establishing position. When it reaches middle shot distance, it stops for a while. Before it again starts to move closer to Axel, there are quick flashbacks of Axel and his mother dancing at the grandfather's party. These flashbacks are also seen from a middle shot distance. The comparative distancing seems appropriate because, psychologically, it stops short of real intimacy. Axel is now remembering his mother in these flashbacks because if he draws a three he should have plenty of money to pay back his debt to her as well as to the syndicate. Still, at the moment when he draws the card, he doesn't want anything to intrude. He wants perfect isolation.

After Axel demands the three from the dealer, a subtle fanfare begins to be heard and the camera starts once more to close in on him. Now, with the camera at a slightly lower angle than before, Reisz creates an exquisitely revealing image. The angling of the camera has appeared to lift Axel up slightly, and it has also forced us to concentrate on his head in perspective to the ceiling. On that ceiling, and now also as if on Axel's head itself, there is a radial light fixture. At the moment when Axel draws the card he demands, the camera holds his face in this perspective, steadily, until it dawns on us that it looks like Axel is wearing a brilliant halo. This lighting effect, joined with James Caan's rapt look of utterly breathless humility, has the appearance of a radiant icon. How very fitting, since to Axel this moment has all the magic which a mystical experience must hold for a saint. And how ironic, since the moment is so full of misguided hope and desire.

Here, incidentally, is one of those points in the film where we can clearly see what Reisz's attitude toward Axel really is. He builds up Axel's magic moment through some fitting imagery because he is really interested in the way a gambler must feel when he wins against the odds. To that extent, Reisz is a sympathetic observer. However, in the end the imagery is so consciously sublime that it ultimately serves to undercut this vision of personal glory.

One additional scene deserves close attention for two good reasons. It works so extremely well and it seems to belong entirely to Reisz. At least there appears no reason to believe that it had to be guided by Toback's original script. Instead, it depends almost exclusively on film style.

It begins with a close-up of a radio broadcasting the basketball game on which Axel has bet all of the money which he still has left from his Las Vegas winnings. In the next shot the camera starts to move slowly past the radio and toward the reflection of Axel in a standing mirror. During this process we hear that there are now only nine seconds left in the game. While those few seconds tick away, however, time seems to be standing still for Axel. This subjective feeling of time is emphasized in two ways. The camera moves up ever so slowly, and the shot is the longest uninterrupted one in the film.

While this markedly long take continues, only James Caan's face seems to be really moving. As a result, every slight move or expression on his face takes on a certain magnitude and dramatic significance. This is why, by watching closely, we can appreciate more fully than anywhere else in the film what he is really going through. Frustration, anxiety, confusion, and anger are all written on his face. It's like seeing a mental battle zone.

When the camera's movement toward Axel stops at mid-close-up, we hear that the game has come down to the last second and the last shot. Naturally Axel's team loses. He then looks simply dazed, and his body sags down slightly. At the same time the sound of the radio announcer's voice begins to trail off until there is a period of silence. Of course, this is subjective silence.

Now two shots isolate first the radio and then Axel. Done in silence, this creates an impression of Axel's great tension. Then this tension snaps, suddenly, as he kicks at the radio. The explosive sound which we then hear is raised purposely in volume. This, effectively, stuns us into imagining how violent and destructive his feelings must be.

Before the scene ends we see Axel's reflection once more in the mirror. We then hear the overlapping sound of a phone. This is followed by a cut to Axel stirring in his bed, groping toward the phone. As he does, the camera begins to slowly pull back, farther and farther. Finally we see the point of this maneuver. Billie has deserted his bed and his apartment. And, we can assume, his life.

The picture of Axel's deserted bed, it should be noted, has a framing function. It is actually a reverse reflection of what we saw just before the scene of Axel's listening to the game begins. At that point he left Billie alone in bed because of his obsession. Now she has left him because of it. That this irony depends on reflective imagery is characteristic of this film. It is a film which is filled with images, parallels, and contrasts which mirror important points. Indeed, it is literally filled with mirrors.

Imagery

Within the radio scene this mirror imagery is so pronounced that it might have become rather forced. This did not happen, however, because of an apparent paradox. Reisz used such a direct approach—simply setting up a mirror and shooting into it—that we don't think much about it after we first discover it. We accept this technique, it seems, because there is no attempt to make us believe that it *hasn't* a symbolic function. We just want the imagery to be truly enlightening. That it is, for the mirror exposes in a trenchant way the nature and the consequences of how Axel looks upon his life. Shot in a very bright light, the scene shows him, clearly, alone with his mania. And this has been done, significantly, without any words from a script really having to be used.

The mirror is the predominant symbolic image in the film. However, there are additional images which also provide the story with an added depth of meaning. Of these the most important have an ironic function. One such image, the halo, has already been mentioned. But related to this idea of self-glorification are several other images which surround Axel. In his apartment there are pictures, posters, and busts of great men. He looks up to them, but he certainly can't measure up to what they stand for. In a way, they are reminders of his failure.

One man who suggests Axel's life of failure most effectively, though, is not a great man at all. As a matter of fact, he is a bum. One day Axel watches him singing, absurdly, "I'm in the mood for love." This picture of Axel watching the bum is full of irony. First, because Axel's sexual advances had just been effectively turned aside by Billie in the previous scene. Second, because the bum's performance may very well be representative of Axel's future. Axel has been seen holding forth with considerable style before the class which he teaches. However, this image of the bum, performing in front of a few old people watching without interest, seems to be there to mock Axel the performer and player.

In this his second color feature, Reisz also uses a variety of interesting color imagery. The three primary colors which he uses are red, green, and black. Red is suggestive mostly of violence. Thus, for example, a strong-arm who picks up Axel to take him to a loan shark, and who then stops on his way to beat up a welshing customer, drives a bright red convertible with his name, Carmine, significantly painted on it. And the prostitute who draws the blood of Axel with the knife wears a dress of the same color. Green is the very first color we see, of course, as the backdrop to the credits. It's the green of the gambling table, and it also stands for the green of money. Therefore, it is fitting that the color of green is often found in the rest of the movie where gambling of various sorts goes on. Black has, principally, the value of corruption. Thus the Harlem pimp, for instance, wears a wholly black outfit. So does the most purely degenerate character in the film, The Monkey. And what does Axel usually wear? Appropriately enough, checks in muted colors to insinuate his complex, divided, and shady nature.

Light and dark imagery are also used with great success. Darkness is used in mostly a traditional way. Usually when the setting is in the underworld of crime or violence it is quite dark and shadowy. Sometimes, however, the darkness of a scene can indicate Axel's subjective fears of corruption. But this corruption is revealed even more effectively through the occasional use of bright lighting. The best example is found in the scene which comes after the point in the story where Axel is frightened into agreeing to try to make his student fix a basketball game. As he walks into the gym where that student is practicing, the initial impression is one of brilliant whiteness. It must seem to Axel that, as he is about to approach the player, all the lights of accusation, of guilt, are trained on him.

What increases this impression is that the previous scene was so very dark. This switching from comparative darkness to lightness is used in other parts of the film. Through this means Reisz creates some forceful tensions. Occasionally he creates such tensions by cutting between comparative loudness in one scene to quietness in the next. But his editing is at those times done with enough subtlety so that we are seduced rather than distracted by the contrasts.

Perhaps there are other things about *The Gambler* which might also be praised. Reisz's "denuded" locations, for example.[11] Or his creation of a particularly oppressive mood. Nevertheless, because of its previously mentioned flaws, *The Gambler* must in the end be judged as one of Reisz's less successful movies.

7

Who'll Stop the Rain

REISZ'S NEXT and most recent film, *Who'll Stop the Rain,* turned out to be one of his better ones. It happens to be true that it is also his most melodramatic film. However, it is far from being just a conventional melodrama. It is instead a symbolic thriller with a lacerating vision of evil. Even a brief plot summary can immediately suggest that it has the elements for a smashing adventure story. But such a summary can also suggest that the story has the elements for the kind of "taut, stringy, *dark* melodrama" Reisz wished to make,[1] for it quickly becomes evident that the central characters are ultimately meant to embody an allegory of a national disaster.

The story begins by focusing on John Converse, a disillusioned war correspondent who decides to get involved in smuggling some heroin from Vietnam home to the United States. His decision has little to do with the money involved. Instead, he sees this as an act of self-assertion and rebellion against a profoundly immoral war. To get the drugs to their destination, he enlists the reluctant help of a friend from his marine days, Ray Hicks, unlike him a man of action. Converse also involves his unwitting wife, Marge, in the plan. He writes her that he is coming home soon, that meanwhile she should expect a friend of his to come by to see her, and that she should have $1,000 ready to give him. On the surface, the plan appears to be safe enough, particularly since he has been assured that important people in the states were behind the drug dealing. However, things go wrong once Hicks arrives at Marge's place. It's bad enough that she has no idea what is going on, and that she doesn't have the money for Hicks. Much worse, though, a corrupt

121

Alone on a windswept beach, fugitives Marge Converse (Tuesday Weld) and Ray Hicks (Nick Nolte) contemplate their next move in Who'll Stop the Rain.

narcotics agent who knows about the shipment has set a trap with two of his thugs.

Hicks, a self-styled samurai, manages to overcome them. However, his and Marge's problems have really just begun. Because they now have been drawn directly into the violent world of drugs, with the heroin still on them, they are in very great danger. Thus they find themselves suddenly running for their lives. While they drive from place to place in search of security and someone who will deal with the drugs, they are pursued by the corrupt agent and his two men. Converse is also with the crooks, although of course unwillingly. He was picked up by them after he had arrived home, tortured, and then brought along on the chase as a possible hostage.

Their pursuers finally catch up with Hicks and Marge on top of a New Mexico mountain. Then violence inevitably breaks loose, and Hicks in the end is one of the dead. Converse and Marge manage to survive, but whether or not their future is safe is another question. The very ending of the film implies that terror, in one form or another, may still await them.

Reisz's Attraction to the Story

The reasons why Reisz was attracted to such a story in the first place are in themselves significant. To begin with, there is Hicks. To Reisz he is the kind of character who has always been fascinating, a kind of modern hero who is doomed. Hicks believes in the values of personal justice, strict loyalty, and action. Action, as a matter of fact, is his primary way of confronting everything, including moral questions. Thus in a sense he is an heir of the virile tradition of the American West. But because he lives in a corrupt new world which appears to be totally hostile to his spiritual ideas, the energy which he expends is destined to lead to disillusionment, then finally to destruction. Therefore, Hicks belongs in a way to the line of Reisz's other central film characters. Like them, he faces the prevailing winds of his time in an absolute, obsessive manner, and those winds overwhelm him, even if perhaps not his spirit.[2]

In expressing additional reasons for his initial attraction to this story, Reisz made two statements which are especially valuable and revealing. They can suggest what the thrust of the film is meant to be. They also tell us something important about the past, ongoing,

and future concerns in his work. In one statement he has said that
he was immediately drawn to the story of *Dog Soldiers*, Robert
Stone's novel on which the film is based, because it was concerned
with a group of characters who "are the products of their time, the
results of the Vietnam war, and thus an authentic portrait of today's
lost generation. The fact that most of the action consists of a chase
is significant because the characters are running away both from
their pursuers and themselves. Their refuge is drugs, violence,
mistrust, and cynicism. They don't like the society that has hurt
them, and they don't like themselves either."[3] Hicks is certainly a
part of this "lost generation." But this statement refers to some
extent even more pointedly to Converse and Marge, for in the story
they clearly come to represent lost people who embody contemporary social issues. Reisz, of course, has dealt with social issues
and psychological misfits of one kind or another in all of his previous
films. Thus, again, *Rain* covers some familiar territory for him. At
the same time, however, the film represents a kind of departure
for Reisz. In another statement where he talks about how he got
into making this film, he recalls that when he read *Dog Soldiers* he
"was immediately attracted to the book because it's a damn good
story. It changes in unexpected ways and takes you into worlds you
didn't know existed—what we used to call a rattling good yarn.
Some of my best experiences in the movie theatre as a viewer have
been with 'The American Storytelling Cinema'—genre films like
*They Live by Night, Force of Evil, Act of Violence, Treasure of the
Sierra Madre*, and a lot of the Ford films. They are defined by
narrative confidence, which is a very American—and not Euro-
pean—tradition. My other films are single-character studies, so I
was very tempted to have a go at one of these."[4]

Script Problems

In having "a go" at it, Reisz followed his stated belief that in
adapting a novel to the screen the filmmaker does himself and the
writer "a favor by making a movie that has its own manner and
integrity and can stand alone." In other words, he thinks of "an
adaptation not as a *translation* but as a variation on a theme."[5] To
a certain extent because of these views, and because Reisz had some
strong opinions about how he wished to treat the story, there were

times when it seemed that the film would never get off the ground. The problem was that, although Reisz felt he knew what he wanted, he had a difficult time finding just the right person with whom he could collaborate on a script.

An account of this search says a great deal about Reisz's determination to find the combination which he believes is right for one of his films. It also may explain why such an organization as United Artists felt that it could work well with him. Evidently because of his careful, assiduous work on *The Gambler,* he had impressed these people. They were, at any rate, remarkably keen on working with him despite the fact that they were certainly aware of the fact that the film had been a failure at the box office. Consequently when Herb Jaffe, an independent producer, came to United Artists with the proposal of turning Stone's novel into a movie, they insisted on Reisz as the director. Jaffe resisted at first because he was afraid of what to him seemed like a "death-wish quality of *The Gambler*— Karel's whole idea in the film of rejecting any kind of commercial pandering."[6] Since United Artists wouldn't, however, hear of someone else as the director of the project, Jaffe made a deal with them which included Reisz.

Jaffe, a commercially shrewd and energetic producer, had good reason to be nervous about working with Reisz. He was right, of course, in his assessment of Reisz's unwillingness to give in to commercial pressures. Moreover, if he consequently suspected as he must have that Reisz was the type of director who might stubbornly insist on having his own way whatever the producer's wishes on a certain important point were, he was right again. Indeed, this is precisely what happened when the two began to talk about hiring a screenwriter.

Jaffe wanted someone other than the author of the novel itself to do the script. Reisz, however, insisted on Stone, whom he had previously met by chance. Thus, as Jaffe recalls, while he was "violently opposed to Stone doing the screenplay," Reisz was just as "violently for him, and it almost became a condition of his being involved with the project."[7] Needless to say, Reisz got his way in the end. But it turned out to be a costly mistake.

For almost a year he and Stone worked on getting something they would both be happy with. Two versions resulted, but neither one would do. The main problem with them turned out to be quite predictable. Stone was so close to his book that he was unwilling to alter it in any significant way. Reisz, on the other hand, felt that several important changes would have to be made because all of the novel's characters and complexities couldn't be transferred successfully to the screen. Besides, he felt that Stone's versions were simply too long. As he saw it, a film based on what Stone had written for him "would have run four hours," and he didn't believe they had "a four-hour story."[8]

Because a kind of stalemate now existed between Stone and Reisz, Jaffe hired Charles Eastman to write a script. He liked the result, a radically altered version. Reisz, however, wasn't pleased with it, and thus he chose Judith Rascoe to give it a try on the strength of a script he had read which she had done for Nicholas Roeg. Fortunately, she turned out to be a good choice. She and Reisz could agree on what was needed, and they collaborated on an adaptation of the novel which was largely faithful to its subject and spirit, although some striking changes were made in the conformation of the story.[9]

The most radical change involved Marge. In the book Marge is involved in the drug scene from the start. In the film, however, she is suddenly pulled into the events because she is vulnerable and naive. Stone has objected that Marge has consequently "been taken off the hook and turned into a kind of innocent in a bid for sympathy that will obviously not be forthcoming. . . ."[10] But Reisz has countered that there were some very good reasons for the change: "We spend time in Vietnam at the beginning of the film, explaining why Converse decides to smuggle the heroin, and we spend the *entire movie* detailing why Hicks cooperates. To take another 15 minutes out to show why Marge gets involved . . . well, the damn thing would have never *started*. So, we had a narrative problem. Secondly, I felt from the point of *drama*—and, of course, the structure of the drama in a film is much different than in a novel—it made a more interesting *equation* to have her innocent and dragged into the scene rather than a willing accomplice."[11]

There is no doubt that Reisz's decision concerning Marge solved some major problems, but it also created a new one which was not entirely resolved. It concerns the relationship which develops between Ray and Marge. In the film the two suddenly undergo a fatal attraction for each other. It may be easy to see why Marge is captivated by Hicks. After all, she is desperately weak and he appears to be so very strong. But what is it that draws him to her and keeps his interest even after, as Andrew Sarris has put it, Marge "degenerates . . . into a nagging bore"?[12] There isn't a clear enough explanation for his infatuation, and thus it seems strangely out of character. At least it seems that way in cold print.

This apparent flaw in the script isn't obvious during the course of the action, however, because of the highly effective pacing and editing of the film and, even more, because of the style Reisz has elected to use.

Film Style

In *Who'll Stop the Rain* all of the major issues of the story are effectively expressed through an appropriate sensory style. For example, the matter of seeing the truth clearly is stressed throughout the film in more ways than one. Most directly, there are a number of characters who are photographed with the glazed eyes of addicts looking at the world and talking about it without much understanding. More subtly, we are made, in a way, to look at these characters and their world through *their* eyes. When this is done, it is largely through the combination of faint, eerie lighting and fast film stock. This method creates a paradoxically ironic effect, a kind of double vision. It gives us the impression of how the world may look to these characters at times—soft, hazy, and mellow, as if lighted by the romantic glow of a nimbus. At the same time, of course, it tells us that these people are blind to some important truths. Ultimately, this technique can make it clearer to us that they are on a dangerous trip where reality and dreams are confounded.

This theme of illusion is expressed even before the start of the opening scene. The film literally begins with an optical illusion, the out-of-focus darkness serving as the background to the credits. As the credits unroll, this background becomes a cloudy mass of sinister shapes. As the credits end, the camera tilts up as if searching for the sky, and the backdrop comes into focus. Then, just when one suspects that the camera eye might be gazing out of a crater, the darkness explodes with light. But it is the ghastly light from a bomb dropped blindly by an American plane on its own side.

In the rest of the movie, light, or the absence of true light, continues to be the dominant and most revealing visual metaphor. Many of the most important scenes actually take place in deep shadow or darkness. In such scenes the shades and shadows which cut the faces of the actors are used in a particularly impressive way, making them resemble apparitions, phantoms surrounded by crepuscular gloom. There are several examples of this effect, but perhaps the first one is the most moving. At the beginning of the film, Converse sits before a letter in which he is trying to tell his wife about his moral crisis. While we listen to his outraged mind in voice-over, we are made to focus on his face in close up. Cut by deep shadows, it stares out through glasses like a specter. Except that this is a human being in a feverish state while recalling some past horrors and looking into what may lie ahead.

Although the movie is generally very dark in look and subject matter, there is a gradual movement from pure darkness to light. We have seen that the film literally begins with total darkness as its background. Then the story moves on under a sky which early in the film is dark with clouds and rain. The story of pursuit which subsequently develops takes place mostly under the black sky of night or under the gray light of smog and haze. Eventually, the sky begins to clear, until at the end light floods the screen. This final light (accentuated through the use of overexposure) is, however, not the light of easy hope but of glaring truth. Serving as the ironic backdrop to the faces of the principal characters, this last light exposes the consequences of their actions. For it consists of a pure, blinding whiteness reflecting the wasteland where they have ended and the drugs which have brought them there.

Questions about the Ending

The last shot of the film, by the way, is a shrewd metaphor of the destiny of Converse and Marge. While the camera holds steady, they drive off into the distance, growing smaller and smaller, almost disappearing as the white sand of the desert and the white sky seem to merge. They appear to have escaped their pursuers. But just how free are they now? Have they actually escaped from their past and the consequences of their actions? Will they now be really able to put their lives back together again? In other words, do we have a "happy" ending in this film?

Since we are dealing with a film by Reisz, the answer is that the ending is characteristically ambiguous. It's not quite as upbeat as

Herb Jaffe, for instance, hoped it would be. While the film was still being shot, he imagined an ending where it is clear that Converse and Marge are "going to make a new life together" because they have learned from their painful mistakes in the recent past.[13] This is close to what Reisz had in mind, since he professed that he wanted an ending which was going to leave the audience "with rather more hope than in the novel."[14] But what he also had in mind was an ending where this hope gave into a certain amount of anguish. As he put it, at the end "Marge and Converse survive, and I want the audience to wish them well. I want the audience to be happy that they survive. This is a paradoxical story: The people who are involved in sending the heroin are the people we are rooting for. It's really a picture about people caught up in an evil time. I think of Marge and Hicks and Converse as all being decent and moral people who are blown by the winds of time. I want the audience to be with them, to think them as fallible and weak like the rest of us."[15] In other words, he meant to have an ending which was, in the last analysis, somewhat rueful and personally unsettling.

That the movie does indeed have this kind of ending is, of course, strongly suggested by the aforementioned wasteland imagery in the very last shot. But it is also emphasized by the title song which comes on at the end. In fact, the meaning of not only the ending but also of the entire story is stressed and made clearer through the use of this song and several other ones heard in the film.

The Use of Music

Before the story concludes, it takes us on a journey through the national psyche which is marked by the moral decadence brought on by the Vietnamese war experience. This decadence is often most effectively expressed through the use of a number of musical pieces. One particularly vivid example of this approach takes place early in the film. It's where some American soldiers talk about catching "gooks" and the best way of killing them. One of these soldiers goes so far as to fantasize "fucking" one of them to death. While this grotesque exchange takes place, a complacent song whines on a radio. Later in the film there are other such examples where the correspondence between what people are saying and doing and what we meanwhile can hear on a radio playing in the background is fiercely ironic.

Another such example actually employs a double irony. It takes place in Los Angeles next to the swimming pool of an apartment complex. In contrast with the preceding scenes, it looks very bright and peaceful. But this is only an illusion. As a matter of fact, it turns out to be the setting for great corruption in the form of a kind of combination pimp and drug pusher who is there. He lies beside a pool like a massive eunuch, voluptuous and inert with self-gratification. A sun reflector directs the light at his face, reflecting the essential truth of his character—blind vanity. In his business he looks down at the weak, self-indulgent "beautiful people" who depend on him to satisfy their base desires. Yet what he won't see is that, in the fullest sense, he is a sinister agent of the American dream which is suffering from corruption. That this is his real significance is stressed by the fact that in the background can be heard the strains of Don McLean's "American Pie," itself a number full of ironic comments about the national loss of innocence.

The movie is, of course, in large part about this loss coupled with the obsessive desire for escape to new experiences. Hank Snow's "Golden Rocket" is used to emphasize this point, once mainly nostalgically, another time ironically. It is first heard during what is the most lyrical, touching scene in the film. While the song plays, Hicks tells Marge about some of his past dreams and hopes. Then, with desperate joy, they dance to the number which wails about getting away. But their fate closes in. Soon after their brief, naive dance, their pursuers catch up with them, and violence follows. This violence explodes with stunning force in a scene taking place in an amphitheater wired for sound. As a possible diversion, Hicks has arranged to have "Golden Rocket" play over the loudspeakers as soon as the expected shooting begins. But when the song begins simultaneously with the shocking violence, it becomes apparent that its message is mocking any effort at escape.

In *Dog Soldiers* there is but one rather offhanded reference to the music of Credence Clearwater Revival, the rock group. Perhaps at first attracted by the ironic resonance of their name, Reisz decided to go further, eventually electing to use three of the group's songs in his movie. As it turned out, this was a fortunate decision for several important reasons. The group happened to be extremely popular during the war years, and thus their music can help recall those times rather automatically for those who lived through them. In addition, because of the nature of the group's music, a combination of intense discord and rude harmony, it corresponds with and adds to the overall complex tone that Reisz was after. Finally, the words of the numbers which are used in the movie certainly help to enrich and clarify the meaning of the story.

The first number, "Proud Mary," is only heard once, and then only briefly. But what is heard is properly ironic. It is the refrain of a quite happy, optimistic song about escaping from the destructive way of life found in the city and finding the good, simple way of life. We hear it, though, while Hicks and Marge are literally on the road to their grim, complex fate.

The second number, "Hey, Tonight," is heard at three different times in the movie, and each time it makes a devastating comment on what is taking place. The first two times, in an infernal bar and on the car radio of Hicks's Landrover, only a portion of the song is heard. The third time, during the shooting scene near the end of the film, we hear the whole piece. It is a strident, coarse, explosive number which is painfully revealing of a national disease. Its first lines show clearly that it is a drug song, but as it screams its decadent message, nobody seems to listen. Or, if they do, they willingly identify with the junkie of the song who shrieks: "Hey, tonight,/Gonna be tonight,/Don't you know I'm buying/Tonight, tonight./Hey, come on,/Gonna chase tomorrow/Tonight, tonight." The bluntest irony of the song is that while it is playing during the shooting scene, Hicks indeed "buys it." Less directly, Reisz uses the song to suggest that his film deals with a whole generation of addicts who are always chasing that impossible tomorrow with a religious fervor.

The third song by Credence Clearwater Revival is the title number, and hence is naturally of greatest significance. The first two times we hear it, Hicks and Marge are on the run. This is appropriate, to begin with, because it is a road song. But not in the sa e way as "Proud Mary." It is not about a way of escape but about entrapment. "Long as I remember," it begins, "The rain's been coming down./Clouds of mist drift, pouring/Confusion on the ground." The search for the metaphorical sun continues throughout the number, but it is not to be found. The refrain of the song asks again and again whether anything can stop the rain (or reign) of darkness and terror. The answer for the main characters seems to be perhaps never, and this frightening possibility is emphasized by the song's slow tempo, heavy with sad harmony, rich with the suggestion of despair.

It is clear, of course, why the film must end with the playing of this number. Without its message, one might misinterpret the significance of the final scene, and thus the point of the story. The last shot of Converse and Marge driving off into an empty landscape already implies that their escape is not perhaps ideal. It is the music, however, which makes the point most emphatically that their future remains full of uncertainty and dread.

The Title

This, incidentally, brings up the point concerning the film's title. A number of critics have complained about the title change from *Dog Soldiers*, with the author himself joining the fray. "I'm pleased with the film," Stone has said, "even though I disagree with the changes in Marge's character and I'm furious about the title change. Hool? Who Will? You can't start a title like that, it sounds like a Lord Buckley routine! It's an absurd, meretricious title and, besides, you can't pronounce it." To this ridiculing objection Herb Jaffe has countered: "I have no second thoughts about changing the title. We tested several titles, including *Running Blind,* and *Dog Soldiers* came out last, especially among women. We want to reach the largest audience possible. You can't make a movie for the purists who bought the book. *Who'll Stop the Rain* was director Karel Reisz's idea. It comes from the Credence Clearwater Revival song that was already in the film and means, 'When is all the suffering and madness going to end?' "[16] As far as Jaffe's box-office hopes were concerned, the retitling seems to have ultimately made little difference. In fact, despite what he had said, he must have had some second thoughts about the title change. After all, when the film eventually played in England it was under the title of *Dog Soldiers.* Nevertheless, there is no denying the fact that the title number fits perfectly into the intricate, allusive overall pattern of the film.

Key Imagery

As has already been pointed out, in the title song as in the film the symbolic quest is for the sun. The rain, however, continues in both. Of course, in the film it literally rains only when Converse goes to pick up the heroin from his contact in Vietnam. In the rest

of the story, though, it rains terror, and this is implied by the fact
that various things keep falling through the air. Most obviously,
there are the bombs of the first scene. But there are also the times
when the camera sits at low angle while helicopters and planes
suddenly drop down from the sky.

The air is also full of disturbing sounds. In fact, as Penelope
Gilliatt suggests, the racket in the movie is so pronounced it is like
a symbolic "rain of noise that this civilization allows to drip so
insistently onto our skulls."[17] That this din is indeed an important
part of the climate of terror is, incidentally, suggested by the very
first sounds we hear. As the credits are about to start, we hear a
low, droning sound. Then as the credits appear one by one against
the sinister background, they are punctuated with violent bolts of
sound. Thus the movie might be said to begin with sounds which
foretell a building storm. Obviously, this is a logical and effective
use of sound imagery since the film is so deeply concerned with
the psychological climate of the characters and the neurotic nation
they represent.

The primary metaphor in the movie is certainly that of heroin.
Therefore, it's not surprising that it accrues a complex meaning
during the course of the story. It is used, for example, to denote
such things as escape, succor, loyalty, and greed.[18] Ultimately, however, its main function is to represent the poisonous influence of
the Vietnamese war and its climate. To stress the point that because
of this obscenity America has become a nation of "junkies," there
is all kinds of trash which the camera picks up. In Vietnam the war
junk seems to be everywhere. In the states trash and junk are also
ubiquitous. A mountain of trash sits in front of the Converses' place.
Their apartment is left in wreckage after a violent struggle takes
place in it. Debris is scattered inside and outside Hicks's hideaway
when he and Marge arrive there. Rubbish clings to fences along
the roads. Meanwhile, people are shooting themselves and each
other in the arm, shoulder, in the buttocks, sometimes with needles
and sometimes with bullets.

This vision of violent decadence is expressed through still other
images and metaphors. But perhaps the single most haunting picture is of Hicks caked with mud after he has made a long run during
an impromptu football game back in Vietnam. He looks one moment
like a dirty kid, the next like a beast of corruption. It is a riveting
film simile. In a highly economical way, Reisz has managed to

suggest that Hicks, starting out as a kind of all-American boy, has embarked on a sordid journey into an underworld he hasn't yet conceived.

Editing and Pacing

The impact of Reisz's infernal vision in this film depends to a great extent on sharp editing. This is especially true of the opening Vietnam sequence where Converse decides to become involved in drug smuggling. This sequence is severely condensed, perhaps to the point where we might at first not be totally satisfied with Converse's words of explanation for his bizarre decision. It doesn't seem *reasonable* enough. On the other hand, because of very effective editing, we can *imagine* what has driven him to his extreme state of mind. As he is pictured agonizing over his letter to his wife, his mental voice tells us about the newest atrocities of the war. While we hear his tortured voice, we also get glimpses of what possesses his mind through several flash cuts. Shot in slow motion, these brief glimpses of the true horror of war seem to hang in suspension. In short, it is a fearful vision, irrational and undeniable, which confronts him and propels him into action.

The editing of the scene where Hicks and his pursuers shoot it out is also very effective. It starts out like the opening scene, with an explosion. Then it is shot from a variety of angles, until the suspicion deepens into an outright awareness that we have seen something like this in the movie before. What it recalls is both a hellish bar scene and, even more decidedly, the opening battle scene where Americans are undergoing a form of self-destruction. When the perspective suddenly cuts back to a long shot, the vision is particularly eerie. Then we hear Hank Snow's recorded voice singing "Golden Rocket" and we see the great darkness punctuated by bursts of light, of fire-power and strobe lights, all purposely combined to create a metaphor for a suicidal culture.

When Hicks gets shot in the shoulder during this violent scene, the movie could have slid into rather crude melodrama. Hicks has told a Mexican friend to wait for him to return to their mountaintop retreat, but how will he make it with his severe wound? Would there now be one of those interminable stretches of abominable suffering and bleeding? Fortunately not. Reisz instead transports

Hicks to the retreat with a brutally quick dissolve, as if to imply that this fanatical man (a reader of Nietzsche, incidentally) has apparently superhuman endurance. And from there he is again suddenly transported, down to the white desert plane where he is supposed to meet up with Converse and Marge but where he is fated to die. It is editing at its best, functional and suggestive of character and theme.

Whenever Reisz decides to depend on longer takes rather than on quick cutting, he can be just as successful. The best example of this approach is found in the scene where Hicks meets Marge for the first time. It is a pivotal scene, since their lives will now become intertwined and since their fates will now be turned around completely. To emphasize this, plus the implicit facts that the two will become the captives of beguilement and fear, Reisz decided to do two things. It would be a long scene, going on for about six pages in the finished script, and it would consist of a single take. But during it, the camera would make a circular pan as it followed Hicks moving around Marge's living room while she watched him.[19] As it turned out, these dynamics were very effective. They managed to call attention to the significance of the scene without diminishing the impression that the story was still hurtling along.

Acting

Who'll Stop the Rain is a most hypnotic film, so that this hurtling sensation, the feeling of being pulled along, is almost constant. On those rare occasions when this impression is spoiled, it's invariably a time when Michael Moriarty as Converse is asked to hold the screen. There is no doubt that Moriarty is a talented actor. He has proved this in a number of other roles. He just doesn't seem right for this part, though. He may look right for it. Certainly his face and bodily movements are appropriately expressive. But there is a serious problem with his voice. Too often it simply tends to betray the wrong things. Perhaps the idea was that his character should use a flat, passionless voice to suggest his moral and psychological despair. Yet even though this idea may work very well in the opening scene where he is thinking out loud about his disillusion, it fails in those parts of the movie where he is confronted not just by his thoughts but by the physical danger of psychotic contempt for life.

The action of *Who'll Stop the Rain* coming to a climax: (top) Antheil (Anthony Zerbe) transmitting instructions to his goons who have caught up with their prey; (bottom) Hicks (Nick Nolte) tells Angel (Joaquin Martinez) about his plans for escaping Antheil's trap.

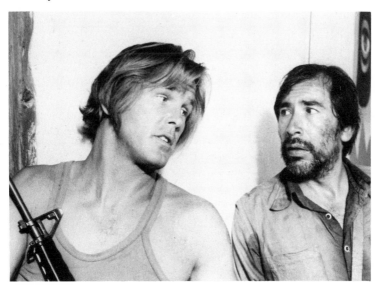

Then he seems to be such a whining Milquetoast that it is hard to feel any real sympathy for him or, worse, even to believe in him.

The rest of the cast, however, is certainly impressive. Tuesday Weld as Marge gives a delicate, touching performance in a role which demands a balancing act between self-pity and self-sacrifice. In the roles of the villains, Anthony Zerbe, Richard Masur, and Ray Sharkey are marvelous as comical, murderous freaks. But it is the performance of Nick Nolte as Hicks which is most remarkable.

To get ready for his part, Nolte worked with great intensity. He lifted weights to get himself in shape physically, for example, and even made himself learn to use a tommy gun. Mentally, he prepared himself by thinking a great deal about his character and then essentially trying to lift him straight from the novel.[20] Once the shooting started, however, there is evidence that Reisz had to tone his obsessive acting down on certain occasions.[21] But only enough so that when Nolte appears on the screen, he has control of his character while still discharging a feeling of special excitement. This excitement takes some unusual forms, since his character is complex and paradoxical. Yet because Nolte manages to seize his role so completely, we have no doubts about the validity of his character while he is on the screen. In fact, one might say that, to a great extent because of the visceral character he creates with the guidance of Reisz, he makes us believe profoundly in this violent, somewhat bizarre, strangely romantic film about human conflict.

8

Concluding Overview and Appraisal

THERE IS NO question that in film criticism the *auteur* theory is the most powerful one today, and with good reason. It has proven again and again that it can be immensely valuable as a critical approach. However, when it comes to applying it systematically to the British scene, it tends to result in some distortions. Seen from the perspective of this theory, the contributions of the most important British filmmakers appear to be less than they really are. Because British films have traditionally been derivative, there appears to be a natural bias built into the *auteur* system against films which are not based on original, personal scripts by their directors.

Reisz, of course, is such a "derivative" filmmaker. All of his feature-length movies are based on the works of other writers. He may have actively collaborated on the scripts at important points along the way, but not at the very beginning. The inspired ideas which initially drive the scripts come from someone else. Thus in the minds of various *auteur* critics he doesn't really qualify as a film author. The politics of film criticism being what they currently are, this notion has become a rather widespread belief. Consequently, he has been relegated to a kind of critical obscurity. He doesn't now interest many critics because they seem to believe that, although he may be a very accomplished, professional director, he can't really be considered as an important artist. Since he only makes adaptations, they feel, he is an interpreter rather than a creator of films.

In a recent interview, Eric Rohmer touched on a point which is exceedingly germane to this issue of film adaptations. As far as he

139

Publicity stills of Karl Reisz rehearsing (top) and shooting on location (bottom) for The Gambler was concerned, he had reached the point where he felt that "the *film d'auteur* was perhaps a myth. Writing a scenario and shooting a film are not only different stages of the film-making process, they are two quite separate acts of creation."[1] Rohmer may, of course, be going too far in suspecting that the *film d'auteur* is but a myth. There seems to be no doubt, however, that he is correct in claiming that a movie results from two distinct stages of creation. In Reisz's case, it is obvious that he plays a supportive role during the first creative stage, the writing of the script. It is equally obvious that he plays an absolutely dominant one during the second, the making of the film. Because his contribution during the second phase is so great, once the film starts to build on the initial scenario, it tends to acquire a new life. Reisz now begins to attune the raw script and a film style, adjusting the two aspects to each other until they have an organic relationship, and until the result fits his creative vision. In other words, until the film becomes his own.

Reisz's best films are those where this process of recreation is most complete. Primarily, this means that in those movies Reisz has gone as far as he can to find a style which appropriately fits and thus brings out the subject of the screenplay. This can be a very complicated process because film style may consist of so many different aspects. The evidence is that Reisz is aware of them all while he is at work. But he tends to focus especially on four—camera style, imagery, sound, and editing.

The Main Components of Style

Robert Bresson once described camera style as a way in which a filmmaker "writes on the screen." That is, he "expresses himself by means of photographed shots of variable length, and from variable angles. On an author worthy of the name, a choice is imposed, dictated by his calculations or his instincts, never by chance. For him, and for him alone, once he has worked out his decoupage, each shot he takes can have only one definite angle, one certain length of time."[2] There seems to be no doubt that this is also how Reisz thinks of camera style. Thus he works very hard to discover the proper one for a particular film. Almost invariably, he has great success. This is why watching one of Reisz's movies can be like a valuable lesson in the proper use of the camera. But one has to watch very closely. Rarely is he blatant or heavy-handed in his choices. Although full of careful strategy, they give the first impression of simply being the most direct, the most functional choices. And this is even true when Reisz doesn't use camera style which is meant to reflect what goes on. That is, when he uses a style which goes against the grain. This happens more frequently than one might at first suppose, for it is usually done with great cunning. At first glance, it is very possible that one might not clearly *see* such an incongruity, or how ironically appropriate it is. One is bound to *feel* it, however. What is then felt, naturally, is that something is out of joint. Needless to say, that is precisely the feeling Reisz wishes to impart. It is one of his ways to make us see, or more precisely sense, that something may be deranged, ironic, or simply wrong in some way. Indeed, it is one of his most effective means of making personal comments in his pictures, of injecting his conscience into them.

Another means is through the use of film imagery, and he is equally effective at this. He has, for example, a wonderful knack for creating sharp, compressed visual compositions which can express simultaneously the interior makeup of the characters and the action which surrounds them. Even more, he knows how to use metaphorical images. This is no small matter. Film does work primarily through visual images. Yet if those images must carry a metaphorical load, they become a very tricky business. As Pier Paolo Pasolini, for example, has pointed out, a metaphor is "an essentially linguistic and literary figure of speech which is difficult to render in the cinema except in extremely rare cases. . . . The cinema represents reality with reality, it is metonymic and not metaphoric."[3] Yet despite the inherent risks, Reisz does use a lot of visual metaphors in his work. The reason why he almost always does so with success is because he selects them so precisely, with the fullest understanding of their nature. What he seems to understand as well as anyone is that the most effective film images have the same fundamental qualities that great poetic images have. They must be so authentic, distinct, and immediate that they manage to organize the complexity of life into sudden visions of harmony. They must give the impression of sense coming out of chaos. That Reisz is conscious of this can be discovered throughout the course of one of his movies. But it is especially evident in the first and the last scenes. There, invariably, Reisz employs images which are extremely eloquent about what the subject of the film is going to be and what one should finally make of it. What we then see has the power of conviction. Reisz's conviction, of course.

What we hear aside from dialogue in one of Reisz's films is also extremely important. In fact, Reisz is a real master at using expressive sound effects and music. This should come as no surprise to anyone who is familar with his book on editing. There he indicated that he had thought a great deal about the full possibilities of the sound medium. What he concluded was that realism was not necessarily the best path which the development of sound should follow. On the contrary, symbolism and expressionism seemed to be more promising directions. Influenced by such pioneers in the experimental use of film sound as Basil Wright and Sergei Eisenstein, he decided that editing sound "to an idea, without respect for the unity of time and space between adjacent shots," could and should be further developed.[4] That he has since followed this experimental path is borne out by his films. It should be emphasized, however, that he doesn't experiment with sound for its own sake. When he uses oblique sound it is because he has determined that it would bring out a point he is trying to make about the story that much more effectively. Typically, though, when he creates such a tension between picture and sound, it's a very subtle one. The result is that the audience is bound to surmise or sense the point rather than "see" it. This is precisely what Reisz is after. Sometimes the indirect way is the best, and it's certainly true of sound. As Reisz knows, it is most telling when used as a medium of evocation rather than statement.

Reisz uses oblique sound with a careful economy. He knows that only certain occasions seem to call for this approach, and that it could easily become distracting if used too frequently. Consequently, when realistic sound works just as well, that is what he prefers to use. It all depends on what kind of mood, tone, or effect is called for. Hence there is often a line of exchange between realistic and expressionistic sound in one of Reisz's movies. If this were done haphazardly, serious problems might of course result. Reisz, however, always plans these tensions out with precision. Thus his goal might be to try to create a rhythmic relationship between the two types of sound. Or he may use the contrasts for shock effect. But whatever he does, it's certain that his ultimate aim is to make sound a part of the stylistic unity he has chosen for his film.

As has been previously noted, the basic style which Reisz employs in one of his pictures is at first inspired by his interpretations of the central character. Then, during the shooting stage, he might try various adjustments for the sake of the stylistic unity he desires. Finally, he tries to rivet everything together during the editing stage. Not surprisingly, he does some of his best work in this area. Having written his important book on editing, he wisely takes his own best advice. Most important, he remembers that "mechanical smoothness is only a secondary factor in good editing. A smooth flow of ideas from shot to shot, that is to say a series of purposeful juxtapositions, is the primary requirement."[5] This kind of relational editing is one of the most expressive aspects of a film by Reisz. Through this means he manages to do a number of revealing things. But his primary ambition for his editing is for it to reflect strongly what he has called a "fundamental artistic aim." This is "to express the feeling and atmosphere rather than simply the facts of a situation. . . ."[6] To see that Reisz is a true expert at such editing all one has to do is watch one of his movies closely. From the standpoint of editing, they all look like exemplary models.

When Reisz's complex stylistics come together successfully, the results can be wonderful. To his credit, they usually do. When they don't, it is because of an inherent problem which resides in his approach to filmmaking. This is that since everything must fit together, if something doesn't, it affects the other components. It's a risk which is constant. If even a minor strand comes loose, a whole scene may begin to unravel. Because he knows this, of course, Reisz takes enormous care to anticipate any possible problem which might spring up.

However, because of this compulsion, another problem may arise. Always there is the risk that, if Reisz plans things out too precisely, he will lose the impression of life that a film must have. What he creates may appear too contrived or analytical. Again, to his credit, this rarely happens. Yet on occasion we may very well become too aware of his stylistic manipulations. Then the worst happens. We cease for a time to believe in the film we are seeing. Or we become conscious that we are after all watching a movie, no longer dreaming that it's real life.

Ironically, there are those critics who have found fault with Reisz for not injecting enough of himself into his movies. They perceive him to be a rather aloof, detached filmmaker. It seems that they have come to this conclusion by focusing especially on his central characters. These are always highly complex people, and consequently of tremendous interest to Reisz. However, this interest is shown by a rather analytical, objective approach to them. In the films, Reisz doesn't take a clear stand for or against them. He remains fascinated and detached at the same time. Because this stand doesn't encourage the audience to identify with the characters, it may leave certain people cold. Yet despite what some critics may think, this is not necessarily a flaw. On the contrary, such an approach to characters can have great merit. It can lead to a fuller understanding of them because it discourages sentimental interpretations. Instead of just an identification with a character, it asks for both an intelligent understanding and a commitment to his problems.

Moral Vision and Theme

This is where Reisz's moral conscience comes in. Like any true artist, he is committed to certain beliefs. These beliefs, as it happens, don't appear to be very complex or radical, but they are honest, they persist, and they inspire his art. In his earlier work one can gather that he was particularly committed to a social revolution which would lower the barriers of the class system in Britain and which would pay more heed to what the spirit of youth and rebellion could teach people about living more vibrantly. This was during what might be called his social realism phase, and it included *We Are the Lambeth Boys* and *Saturday Night and Sunday Morning*. But already in *Saturday Night* what eventually became Reisz's major theme in the rest of his work is apparent. In that movie the central character dares to be different, to stand outside society, to be a stranger. There might be something heroic in this but, unfortunately, such a person is doomed in our age. The forces of normal, safe society are too powerful for him in the end, however obsessed he is with confronting them. Thus the inevitable end for such a character is destruction, conformity, or madness. In the case of Arthur Seaton, the end is a kind of mad conformity. But in Reisz's subsequent films, madness, especially romantic madness, appears more and more directly and frequently as the thematic consequence. Or, at any rate, in all of the movies which follow the central characters are in some way existing between sanity and madness because they stand outside the confining borders of social conformity.

Why has this become Reisz's major theme? No doubt it has a great deal to do with the events of his childhood which uprooted him from his native land and his parents. Being a displaced person, he was bound to take a natural interest in others who are outsiders or don't belong in some way. This, in turn, must bear on the pessimistic view of the world which possesses Reisz like so many other intelligent human beings who have thought deeply about the modern world. In such a world, people are continuously driven to the brink by various pressures. How they respond is what is significant. Clearly, this is of primary interest in all of Reisz's films.

It should be stressed that Reisz doesn't pretend that he has any new advice which might save us from the various threats and pressures which seem to be everywhere. He does want us to realize what they are. However, that may be the most he can do, he seems to be saying. Thus all of his movies end in a kind of hopelessness. In other words, there are no "happy" endings. Of course, there is the ending of *Morgan!*, which is filled with laughter. But what is the joke? Morgan is in a lunatic asylum. It appears, therefore, to be Reisz's way of saying that insanity may be the only way to escape from this crazy, painful world.

How, then, can we *face* this world? Reisz's way seems to be made up of a combination of irony and commiseration. The world is full of absurdities, many of them dangerous, and we may as well see them for what they are. If we can look at them ironically, they appear less threatening. We will then at least retain a poise, a dignity, which can give us strength. Besides, if we really face the world in such a way, we can see that we are not alone. This is, of course, a form of comfort. It is also a reason for caring for others, and for trying to understand the reasons for their actions, however alien or unsettling they may appear to us at first.

Reisz's vision, then, is realistic in the fundamental sense. If he prefers to center on characters who are marked by abnormal psychology, it's because they can attract our attention to their real problems so dramatically. In a certain way, they are symbolic characters. But like the best symbols, they are grounded on the natural facts of life. This is why they can make us effectively see the world for what it is, and not just what it seems to be. At the very least, they can express what the world looks like to Reisz.

Contributions to Film Art

Reisz's vision may at first appear to be more complex than it actually is because of his eclectic style. He is not a strict expressionist, symbolist, or realist in his film language. He uses whatever he decides works best at a particular time. However, such a choice is never made in a vacuum. A stylistic choice has to be right for the moment and for the whole picture. Because he is such a master at this, he is of importance to anyone who is interested in the artistic possibilities of film.

Historically, he is important as well. His book on editing is still one of the most useful cinema books in existence. Any aspiring filmmaker would certainly do well to read it. In fact, anyone who wishes to simply learn more about how pieces of film can create a whole new world can learn a great deal from it.

In the realm of documentary, Reisz also has a significant place. As part of the "Free Cinema" movement, he helped to create an atmosphere which led to a resurgence of the great documentary tradition of Britain. In addition, he turned out to be one of the forerunners of what is now known as direct cinema.[7]

As far as his feature films are concerned, he has certainly left his mark. There is a consensus that *Saturday Night and Sunday Morning* is not only one of the best movies to come out of British social realism, but that it is the classic of the movement. *Morgan!*, on the other hand, is widely perceived as a classic of the 1960s film scene in Britain. Perhaps better than any other film, it captures the spirit and the style of that era. Of *Isadora* it must be said that it is simply one of the best film biographies yet made. And as for *Who'll Stop the Rain*, there is reason to believe that it will eventually be recognized as one of the most significant films made about the Vietnamese war era.

Finally, something should be said about the acting in Reisz's movies. In all of them, he works closely with the members of the cast. Thus a kind of collaboration invariably takes place. The actors, of course, come to depend especially on the force of his vision.

Reisz, meanwhile, depends on them in two primary ways. To begin with, he decides on the final composition of a scene only after he has imagined his particular actors in the context, and generally only after he has actually had pertinent discussions with them. In addition, he depends on them to a certain extent for the sense of spontaneity he always strives for. In this connection, Reisz purposely tries to start with a scenario so rigid that it directly challenges the actors to tone down and make it more flexible through their natural instincts. [8]

Largely because of this kind of challenging, productive collaboration, Reisz's films are distinguished by some very great acting. Most obviously, there are the performances of Albert Finney in *Saturday Night,* David Warner in *Morgan!,* and Vanessa Redgrave in *Isadora.* They are simply marvelous in their roles. Exactly how much credit should go to Reisz is of course impossible to say. There is no doubt, however, that he is the type of director who takes the lead and insists in his characteristically quiet way on perfection. That he usually gets what he wants is borne out by various statements from his performers and by his cumulative work.

What's Next?

At the present time Reisz is in the midst of working on his next project, an adaptation of John Fowles's *The French Lieutenant's Woman.* Of course, it's always dangerous to speculate about the future. Nevertheless, there is good reason to hope that this new film will add to Reisz's stature. It's based on just the kind of work which is bound to challenge his best instincts, a work which is highly complex, elusive, and full of human entanglements. Moreover, at last report, the script for the movie was to be done by Harold Pinter, certainly a writer who should work well with Reisz since they both have such a penchant for the intricate, suggestive, and ironic approach to their subject matter.

Whatever the fate of *The French Lieutenant's Woman* turns out to be, Reisz should be able to look forward to a number of productive years yet ahead of him. He is, after all, still very much in his prime. But even if for some reason his career were to come to an end now, he would have already left his imprint on film history. This is because, more than anything else, he has created a body of work which exhibits, often brilliantly, the remarkable expressive power and the enormous artistic potential of the medium. In short, his work reveals that he possesses an extraordinary feeling for his art, and that consequently he must be seen as a truly great film stylist.

Notes and References

Chapter One

1. Much of this kind of primary biographical information comes from a letter written to me by Karel Reisz on November 9, 1979.

2. Michel Ciment, "Nouvel Entretien avec Karel Reisz," *Positif* 212 (November 1978): 17.

3. Reisz and Anderson, by the way, continued to stay close, and about ten years later they collaborated on another project. This time Reisz produced Anderson's 1963 film, *This Sporting Life*.

4. Letter from Reisz.

5. Thorold Dickinson, "Introduction," *The Technique of Film Editing*, by Karel Reisz (London: Focal Press and W. & J. MacKay and Co., Ltd., 1958), p. 7.

6. Reisz has indicated that one thing he has continued to learn from making commercials (which he has been making through the years as a means of livelihood) is to create images which are so highly condensed and disciplined that they are not only functional but also charged with suggestive meaning.

7. Liz-Anne Bawden, ed., *The Oxford Companion to Film* (New York: Oxford University Press, 1976), p. 268. Robert Vas was another of these young filmmakers. His "Free Cinema" contribution, *Refuge England*, inspired by the fact that he was a Hungarian in exile, was critically well received. But he continued to live in relative obscurity until he died in 1977. The next year Reisz made a film for television which commemorated this documentarist.

8. Alexander Walker, *Hollywood, U.K.: The British Film Industry in the Sixties* (New York: Stein and Day, 1974), p. 26.

9. Ibid., p. 36.

10. Ibid., p. 29.

149

11. Lewis Jacobs, "New Trend in British Documentary: Free Cinema," *The Documentary Tradition*, ed. Lewis Jacobs (New York: W. W. Norton & Company, 1979), p. 335.

12. Gavin Lambert, "Free Cinema," *Sight and Sound* 25 (Spring 1956): 176.

13. Ibid.

14. Richard Hoggart, "We Are the Lambeth Boys," *Sight and Sound* 28 (Summer-Autumn 1959): 164–65.

15. Walker, p. 38.

16. Ibid.

Chapter Two

1. Walker, p. 38.

2. Ibid., p. 82.

3. Ibid.

4. Ibid.

5. Ibid.

6. Ibid.

7. Ibid.

8. Boleslaw Sulik, "Saturday Night and Sunday Morning," *Masterworks of the British Cinema* (New York: Harper and Row, 1974), p. 351.

9. Pauline Kael, "Commitment and the Straitjacket," *I Lost It at the Movies* (Boston: Little, Brown and Company, 1965), p. 74.

10. Walker, p. 85.

11. Ibid.

12. Ibid.

13. Ibid., p. 89.

14. Ibid., p. 83.

15. Ibid.

Chapter Three

1. Walker, p. 89.

2. Ibid., p. 147.

3. Ibid.

4. Ibid., p. 148.

5. Ibid.

6. Ibid., pp. 148–49.

7. Gene D. Phillips, "An Interview With Karel Reisz," *Cinema/Los Angeles* (Summer 1968), p. 53.

8. Walker, p. 149.

9. Ibid.

Chapter Four

1. Roger Manvell, *New Cinema in Britain* (New York: E. P. Dutton and Co., Inc., 1969), pp. 8–9.
2. Ibid., p. 98.
3. Walker, p. 310.
4. Dwight MacDonald, "Films," *Esquire* 66 (October 1966): 46.
5. Brendan Gill, "Song of Kong," *New Yorker*, April 9, 1966, p. 88.
6. Pauline Kael, "So Off-Beat We Lose the Beat," *Kiss Kiss, Bang Bang* (Boston: Little, Brown and Co., 1968), p. 21.
7. Ibid.
8. Karel Reisz, *The Technique of Film Editing* (London: Focal Press and W. & J. Mackay and Co., Ltd., 1958), p. 102.
9. Walker, p. 311.
10. Ibid.
11. Ibid.
12. Kael, *Kiss Kiss, Bang Bang*, p. 23.
13. David Paletz, "Morgan," *Film Quarterly* (Fall 1966), pp. 54–55.
14. Walker, p. 310.
15. Ibid., p. 311.
16. Jay Leyda, ed., *Voices of Film Experience* (New York: Macmillan Publishing Co., Inc., 1977), pp. 380–81.
17. Paletz, p. 53.
18. Walker, p. 312.

Chapter Five

1. Louis Untermeyer, *Makers of the Modern World* (New York: Simon and Schuster, 1966), p. 522.
2. Ibid., p. 532.
3. Stephen Farber, "Artists in Love and War," *Hudson Review* 22 (Summer 1969): 295.
4. Estelle Changas, "Isadora," *Film Quarterly* (Summer 1969), p. 46.
5. Gordon Gow, "Isadora," *Films and Filming* (May 1969): 53.
6. Changas, pp. 45–46.
7. Doris Hering, "The Loves of Isadora," *Dance Magazine* (June 1969): 29.
8. When *Isadora* came out, it was inevitably compared with Ken Russell's 1966 television film about the dancer. Russell's exuberant, baroque, and typically eccentric approach, mixed with a semidocumentary style, scored well with many people. One of these was Reisz himself. In responding to the point that his and Russell's films are frequently compared, he recently said: "I liked Ken's film very much. It was very much a film about the '20s. He's great at evoking an epoch and an ambiance. We were going

for the dancing, for the inwardness of the character. People do compare things, but it's quite irrelevant to one's own work. I don't see why people shouldn't like or dislike both." Gordon Gow, "Outsiders: Karel Reisz in an Interview with Gordon Gow," *Films and Filming* (January 1979), p. 16.

Chapter Six

1. Jean-Paul Törörk, "Entretien avec Karel Reisz," *Positif* 212 (November 1978): p. 6.
2. Ibid.
3. Ibid.
4. Robert Chartoff and Irwin Winkler, "Dialogue on Film," *American Film*, December–January 1977, p. 40.
5. Michael Dempsey, "The Gambler," *Film Quarterly* (Spring 1975): 52.
6. Török, pp. 8, 10.
7. Pauline Kael, "The Actor and the Star," *Reeling* (New York: Warner Books, 1976), p. 467.
8. Arthur Cooper, "Winner Take All," *Newsweek*, October 7, 1974, p. 95.
9. Kael, *Reeling*, pp. 467–68.
10. Török, pp. 7, 8.
11. John Coleman, "Bitter Rice," *New Statesman*, April 11, 1975, p. 492.

Chapter Seven

1. Leigh Charlton, "Who'll Stop the Director?" *Village Voice* 23 (September 4, 1978): 63.
2. Michel Ciment, "Nouvel Entretien avec Karel Reisz," *Positif* 212 (November 1978): 12, 13, 15.
3. Betty Jeffries Demby, "Cannes 1978," *Filmmakers Newsletter*, September 1978, p. 64.
4. Charlton, p. 63.
5. Ibid.
6. Stephen Zito, "*Dog Soldiers:* Novel into Film," *American Film*, September 1977, p. 10.
7. Ibid.
8. Ibid., p. 12.
9. Ibid., p. 10.
10. Charlton, p. 62.
11. Ibid.
12. Andrew Sarris, "Getting Stoned on Dope and Dogma," *Village Voice* 23 (September 4, 1978): 63.

13. Zito, p. 10.
14. Ibid., p. 13.
15. Ibid.
16. Charlton, p. 62.
17. Penelope Gilliatt, "Din," *New Yorker*, September 4, 1978, p. 94.
18. Ciment, p. 13.
19. Zito, p. 11.
20. Ibid., p. 13.
21. Ibid., p. 11.

Chapter Eight

1. Gilbert Adair, "Rohmer's *Perceval*," *Sight and Sound* 47 Autumn 1978, p. 231.
2. John Russell Taylor, *Cinema Eye, Cinema Ear* (New York: Hill and Wang, 1964), p. 124.
3. John Russell Taylor, *Directors and Directions* (New York: Hill and Wang, 1975), p. 172.
4. Reisz, *The Technique of Film Editing*, p. 66.
5. Ibid., p. 232.
6. Ibid., p. 142.
7. Richard Meran Barsam, *Nonfiction Film* (New York: E. P. Dutton and Co., Inc., 1973), p. 237.
8. Ciment, p. 18.

Selected Bibliography

Primary Sources

1. Book

The Technique of Film Editing. London: Focal Press and W. and J. Mackay and Co., Ltd., 1958. This is Reisz's classic book on film editing. After it became clear that some additions would have to be made to cover some revolutionary practices that subsequently arose in filmmaking, Gavin Millar added a section to an enlarged edition (1968).

2. Screenplays

Morgan! London: Calder and Boyars, 1966.

Saturday Night and Sunday Morning, in *Masterworks of British Cinema*. New York: Harper and Row, 1974. With three scripts from other films not directed by Reisz.

Note: The British Film Institute houses the scripts of *We Are the Lambeth Boys* and *Saturday Night and Sunday Morning*, along with the play on which *Morgan!* is based.

Secondary Sources

ADAIR, GILBERT. "Rohmer's *Perceval*," *Sight and Sound* 47 (Autumn 1978): 230–34. Eric Rohmer makes some personal comments about the stages of filmmaking which seem to apply to Reisz's experience as well.

ANDREW, J. DUDLEY. *The Major Film Theories*. New York: Oxford Univ. Press, 1976. A helpful summary of the main film theories put into functional prose.

ANONYMOUS. "Desert Island Films," *Films and Filming* 9 (August 1963): 11–13. Reisz lists his ten favorite films.

———. "From Free Cinema to Feature Film," *The Times* (London), May

19, 1960, p. 18. One of the first, and still one of the very few, interviews which Reisz has given or which exist in print.

———. "How to Get into Films—By the People Who Got in Themselves," *Films and Filming* 9 (July 1963): 11–14. Reisz briefly recounts how he got into the filmmaking business.

———. "Karel Reisz: Free Czech," *Films and Filming* 7 (February 1961): 5. A brief life and career sketch of Reisz up to *Saturday Night and Sunday Morning*.

———. "Mad about the Boy," *Time*, June 24, 1966, p. 80. An attempt to explain why Morgan, the character of the movie, seemed to be so popular with the female audience.

ARMES, ROY. *A Critical History of the British Cinema.* New York: Oxford Univ. Press, 1978. Provides a brief sketch of Reisz's career and some of his accomplishments, but it's not a very helpful book when it comes to a critical look at Reisz's individual films.

BARSAM, RICHARD MERAN. *Nonfiction Film.* New York: E. P. Dutton and Co., Inc., 1973. This book contains a disappointingly sketchy look at the "Free Cinema" people and their work.

CHANGAS, ESTELLE. "Isadora," *Film Quarterly* (Summer 1969), pp. 45–48. A rigorous and incisive analysis of the film.

CHARLTON, LEIGH. "Who'll Stop the Director," *Village Voice* 23 (September 4, 1978): 62–63. A valuable article because of the comments made by novelist and director about what they thought of adapting *Dog Soldiers* into *Who'll Stop the Rain.*

COLEMAN, JOHN. "Bitter Rice," *New Statesman*, April 11, 1975, p. 492. A mixed review which rightly complains that *The Gambler* seems a "shade too literate."

COOPER, ARTHUR. "Winner Take All," *Newsweek*, October 7, 1974, pp. 95–96. This review focuses mainly on the acting in *The Gambler.*

CUTTS, JOHN. "Night Must Fall," *Films and Filming* 10 (June 1964): 21–22. Focus on some of the flaws which exist in Reisz's second feature film.

DEMBY, BETTY JEFFRIES. "Cannes 1978," *Filmmakers Newsletter* 11 (September 1978): 60–64. Contains a significant comment by Reisz as to why he was attracted to making *Who'll Stop the Rain.*

DEMPSEY, MICHAEL. "The Gambler," *Film Quarterly* 28 (Spring 1975): 49–54. A balanced analysis of the film's strengths and weaknesses.

DURGNAT, RAYMOND. "Morgan—A Suitable Case for Treatment," *Films and Filming* 12 (June 1966): 6, 10. Durgnat complains about what he considers to be the film's confused style.

DYER, PETER JOHN. "Saturday Night and Sunday Morning," *Sight and Sound* 30 (Winter 1960–61): 33. An astute review of some of the real distinctions of Reisz's first feature film.

FARBER, STEPHEN. "Artists in Love and War," *Hudson Review* 22 (Summer 1969): 295–306. This essay is especially important because it attempts

to discuss *Isadora* from the standpoint of how it was meant to be seen
before it was so drastically cut.

GILL, BRENDAN. "Song of Kong," *New Yorker*, April 9, 1966, pp. 86, 88,
91. This is one of the more positive reviews of *Morgan!*

GILLIATT, PENELOPE. "Din," *New Yorker*, September 4, 1978, pp. 94–95.
A penetrating review which focuses on Reisz's use of expressive sound
in *Who'll Stop the Rain.*

———. "Feet," *New Yorker*, April 26, 1969, pp. 85–86, 91–92, 94. Praise
for *Isadora* as film biography.

GOW, GORDON. "Isadora," *Films and Filming* (May, 1969), pp. 52–53. A
mixed review of *Isadora.*

———. "Outsiders: Karel Reisz in an Interview with Gordon Gow," *Films
and Filming* (January 1979), pp. 13–17. One of the fullest treatments
of Reisz's career available thus far. It's especially valuable for what
Reisz has to say about his interest in characters who stand outside
"normal" society.

HERING, DORIS. "The Loves of Isadora," *Dance Magazine*, June 1969, pp.
29–30, 78–80. This is a valuable essay primarily because it gives one
the perspective of Vanessa Redgrave's performance as Isadora Duncan
from the dancing standpoint.

HOGGART, RICHARD. "We Are the Lambeth Boys," *Sight and Sound* 28
(Summer-Autumn 1959): 164–65. This is still the most complete and
incisive article on "We Are the Lambeth Boys" and one of the more
valuable essays on "Free Cinema" as well.

KAEL, PAULINE. "Commitment and the Straitjacket," *I Lost it at the Movies*. Boston: Little, Brown and Company, 1965. pp. 62–78. In this
essay (focusing on *Saturday Night and Sunday Morning*) and in those
from the books listed below, Kael may sometimes be off the mark,
particularly when her enthusiasm carries her away. However, these
are some of the more important essays on Reisz because, at the very
least, they are so thought-provoking.

———. "So Off-Beat We Lost the Beat," *Kiss Kiss, Bang Bang*. Boston:
Little, Brown and Company, 1968, pp. 20–25. Kael focuses on *Morgan!*

———. "The Actor and the Star," *Reeling*. Boston: Little, Brown and
Company, 1976, pp. 465–73. Kael focuses on *The Gambler.*

KAUFFMANN, STANLEY. "Later On," *New Republic*, September 30, 1978,
pp. 26–27. An attempt to put Reisz's career in perspective while re-
viewing *Who'll Stop the Rain.* But what mainly seems to come out is
that Kauffmann wishes that Reisz might have been allowed to keep
making versions of *Saturday Night and Sunday Morning.*

LAMBERT, GAVIN. "Free Cinema," *Sight and Sound* 25 (Spring 1956):
173–77. Still the single best article on what "Free Cinema" was all
about.

LEYDA, JAY, ed. *Voices of Film Experience.* New York: Macmillan Publishing Co., Inc., 1977. This book quotes briefly such people as Reisz and Vanessa Redgrave about their work in films.

MACDONALD, DWIGHT. "Films," *Esquire* 66 (October 1966): 40, 42, 44, 46, 185. One of the more negative reviews of *Morgan!* MacDonald objects particularly to what he sees as the chaotic mixture of style and point of view.

MANVELL, ROGER. *New Cinema in Britain.* New York: E. P. Dutton and Co., Inc., 1969. This pictorial book which deals with British movies after World War II and up to 1969 is too sketchy to be of value other than as an introduction and a quick survey.

PALETZ, DAVID. "Morgan," *Film Quarterly* (Fall 1966), pp. 51–55. One of the more carefully analytical essays on *Morgan!*

PHILLIPS, GENE D. "An Interview with Karel Reisz," *Cinema/Los Angeles,* Summer 1968, pp. 53–54. Rather sketchy and thin in content, but still of value because it is one of the rare interviews which Reisz has given.

PYM, JOHN. "Dog Soldiers," *Sight and Sound* 48 (Winter 1978–79): 58–59. Pym argues that, although *Who'll Stop the Rain* starts out well, it loses direction once the story takes the characters on the road.

SARRIS, ANDREW. "Getting Stoned on Dope and Dogma," *Village Voice* 23 (September 4, 1978): 63, 65. An impressionistic review which asks some pointed questions about character motivation but is ultimately disappointing because it actually only drifts over the surface of the film's art and finally leaps to a personal view on the legalization of drugs!

SCHICKEL, RICHARD. "Mad Fantasy," *Time,* October 28, 1974, p. 5. Finds fault with *The Gambler,* including Caan's performance.

————. "The Brilliant Biog. of Isadora D.," *Life,* April 18, 1969, p. 12. High praise for *Isadora* as a film biography.

————. "There, There Little Non-Hero," *Life,* May 6, 1966, p. 16. One of the more unfavorable reviews of *Morgan!*

————. "Wasted," *Time,* August 21, 1978, p. 52. Schickel concludes in his brief review that *Who'll Stop the Rain* is "just another ambitious downer."

SIMON, JOHN. "Films," *Esquire* (November 1974), pp. 44, 46, 50, 101. Finds fault with, among other things, the tempo of *The Gambler.*

SULIK, BOLESLAW. "Saturday Night and Sunday Morning," *Masterworks of the British Cinema.* New York: Harper and Row, 1974, pp. 348–52. A valuable overview of Reisz's first feature film, the script of which is one of the "masterworks" included in this book. It also contains a helpful introductory essay on the character of British film by John Russell Taylor.

SUTHERLAND, ELIZABETH. "Saturday Night and Sunday Morning," *Film Quarterly* (Summer 1961), pp. 58–59. Has some important insights into the expressive use of sound in Reisz's first feature film.

TÖRÖK, JEAN-PAUL. "To Stand Outside and Risk," *Positif* 212 (November 1978): 2–3. The first of several pieces dedicated to Reisz in this issue of *Positif.* Included in this issue are two interviews with Reisz. Invaluable for anyone doing serious research on this director. In French.

UNTERMEYER, LOUIS. *Makers of the Modern World.* New York: Simon and Schuster, 1966. Untermeyer has a concise, revealing chapter on the life and character of Isadora Duncan, pp. 522–32.

WALKER, ALEXANDER. *Hollywood, U.K.: The British Film Industry in the Sixties.* New York: Stein and Day, 1974. This is the best work on the British film scene beginning with the "Free Cinema" movement and continuing into the early 1970s. As the title suggests, it deals with the business side of the scene. But it also focuses critically on the major films during the span it covers. In the process it becomes a kind of social history, too. The book gets much of its life from the many interviews with filmmakers which Walker held.

ZITO, STEPHEN. "*Dog Soldiers:* Novel into Film," *American Film,* September 1977, pp. 8–15. Zito visited the set while *Who'll Stop the Rain* was being made, interviewed most of the important contributors, and then wrote an essay which is especially significant for the light it casts on how Reisz works and what some of the production problems and thematic intents of the film were.

Filmography

MOMMA DON'T ALLOW (British Institute, Experimental Film Fund, 1956)
Codirector: Tony Richardson
Photography: Walter Lassally
Editing/Sound: John Fletcher
Music: The Chris Barber Band, with Chris Barber (trombone), Pat Halcox (trumpet), Monty Sunshine (clarinet), Lonnie Donnegan (guitar), Jim Bray (counterbase), Ron Bowden (drums), Ottilie Patterson (singing)
Running Time: 22 minutes

WE ARE THE LAMBETH BOYS (Graphic Films, for the Ford Motor Company, 1959. Second film of the series "Look at Britain")
Executive Producer: Robert Adams
Producer: Leon Clore
Assistants: Louis Wolfers, Raoul Sobel
Photography: Walter Lassally
Editing: John Fletcher
Music: John Dankworth and his orchestra.
Commentary: John Rollason
Running Time: 52 minutes
16mm Rental: Contemporary Films/McGraw-Hill

SATURDAY NIGHT AND SUNDAY MORNING (Woodfall Film Productions, 1960)
Producer: Tony Richardson
Executive Producer: Harry Saltzman
Screenplay: Alan Sillitoe
Photography: Freddie Francis

Cameraman: Ron Taylor
Art Direction: Lionel Couch
Set Decoration: Timothy O'Brien
Editing: Ted Marshall, Seth Holt
Music: John Dankworth and his orchestra
Sound: Peter Handford, Bob Jones
Sound Editing: Chris Greenham
Assistant Director: Tom Peysner
Production Director: Jack Rix
Cast: Albert Finney (Arthur Seaton), Shirley Anne Field (Doreen Gretton),
    Rachel Roberts (Brenda), Hylda Baker (Aunt Ada), Norman Rossington
    (Bert), Bryan Pringle (Jack), Robert Cawdron (Robboe), Edna Morris
    (Mrs. Bull), Elsie Wagstaff (Mrs. Seaton), Frank Pettit (Mr. Seaton),
    Avis Bunnage, Colin Blakely, Irene Richmond, Louise Dunn, Peter
    Madden, Cameron Hall, Alister Williamson, Anne Blake
Running Time: 89 minutes
16mm Rental: Budget

NIGHT MUST FALL (Metro-Goldwyn-Mayer Pictures, 1964)
Producers: Albert Finney, Karel Reisz
Executive Producer: Laurence P. Bachman
Screenplay: Clive Exton
Photography: Freddie Francis
Cameraman: Gerry Fischer
Art Direction: Lionel Couch
Set Decoration: Timothy O'Brien
Editing: Fergus McDonell, Philip Barnikel
Music: composed and directed by Ron Grainer
Sound Editing: Malcolm Cooke
Mixing: J. B. Smith
Assistant Director: David Tomblin
Production Director: Tomothy Burrill
Cast: Albert Finney (Danny), Mona Washbourne (Mrs. Bramson), Susan
    Hampshire (Olivia), Sheila Hancock (Dora), Michael Medwin (Derek),
    Joe Gladwin (Dodge), Martin Wyldeck (Inspector Willet), John Gill
    (Foster)
Running Time: 101 minutes.
16mm Rental: Films Incorporated

MORGAN! (Quintra Productions, British Lion Films, 1966)
Producer: Leon Clore
Screenplay: David Mercer

Photography: Larry Pizer, Gerry Turpin
Art Direction: Philip Harrison
Editing: Victor Proctor, Tom Priestley
Music: John Dankworth
Sound: Peter Handford
Assistant Director: Claude Watson
Production Director: Roy Baird
Cast: Vanessa Redgrave (Leonie Delt), David Warner (Morgan Delt), Robert Stephens (Charles Napier), Irene Handl (Mrs. Delt), Newton Blick (Mr. Henderson), Nan Munro (Mrs. Henderson), Bernard Bresslaw (policeman), Arthur Mullard (Wally), Graham Crowden (lawyer), Peter Cellier, John Rae, Angus MacKay, Peter Collingwood, John Garrie, Marvis Edwards, Robert Bridges
Running Time: 97 minutes
16mm Rental: Cinema 5

ISADORA (Universal, 1968)
Producers: Robert and Raymond Hakin
Screenplay: Melvyn Bragg, Clive Exton
Added Dialogue: Margaret Drabble
Adaptation: Melvyn Bragg
Photography: Larry Pizer
Cameraman: Denis Lewiston
Art Direction: Michael Seymour, Miso Senesis, Ralph Brinton
Assistant Art Director: Roger King
Set Decoration: Bryan Graves, Harry Cordwell, Jocelyn Herbert
Editing: Tom Priestley
Assistant Editor: Philip Baker
Music: Original music composed and conducted by Maurice Jarre; music for the modern dance sequences composed by Anthony Bowles; music for the classic dance sequences arranged and conducted by Anthony Bowles
Choreography: Litz Pisk
Sound: Ken Ritchie, Maurice Askew
Sound Editing: Terry Rawlings
Assistant Directors: Claude Watson, Grania O'Shannon, Adrian Hughes
Supervisor of Production: Roy Parkinson
Director of Production: Eric Rattray
Director of Production in Yugoslavia, Italy, and France: Henri Baum
Cast: Vanessa Redgrave (Isadora), John Fraser (Roger), James Fox (Gordon Craig), Jason Robards (Paris Singer), Ivan Tchenko (Essenine), Vladimir Leskova (Bugatti), Cynthia Harris (Mary Desti), Bessie Love (Mrs. Duncan), Tony Vogel (Raymond Duncan), Libby Glenn (Eliz-

abeth Duncan), Ronnie Gilbert British (Miss Chase), Wallas Eaton (Archer), Nicholas Pennel (Bedford), John Quentin (Pim), Christian Duvaleix (Armand), David Healy (manager of Chicago theater), Lucinda Chambers (Deirdre), Simon Lutton Davies (Patrick), Noel Davis (doctor), Ina De La Haye (Russian teacher), John Brandon (Gospel Billy), Constantine Yranski, Stefan Gryss, Margaret Courtenay, Arthur White, Iza Teller, John Warner, Alan Gifford, Zuleika Robson, Arnold Diamond, Anthony Gardner, Sally Travers, Mark Dignam, Robin Lloyd, Lucy Saroyan, Jan Conrad, Hal Galili, Roy Stephens, Cal McCord, Richard Marner
Running Time: 136 minutes (the original, premiering in Los Angeles in September 1968, was 177 minutes long)
16mm Rental: Twyman Films

ON THE HIGH ROAD (Made for BBC television, 1973)
Producers: Gavin Millar, Melvyn Bragg
Assistant Director: Jerry Harrison
Screenplay, English Adaptation: Jeremy Brooks, Kitty Hunter Blair from a story by Chekhov
Photography: Brian Tufano
Music Arrangement: Anthony Bowles; accordion by Henry Krein
Editing: David Martin
Design: Tony Abbott
Costumes: Robin Fraser-Paye
Sound: Michael Turner, Stan Morcomb
Cast: Colin Blakely (Merik), Graham Crowden (Bortsov), David Baker (Fedya), Bob Hoskins (Kuzma), Barry Keegan (Tikhon), Peter Madden (Savva), Vanda Godsell (Maria), Lucy Griffiths (Efimova), Natalie Kent (Nazarovna), Jimmy Gardner (a traveller), David Sterne (coachman)
Running Time: 47 minutes

THE GAMBLER (Paramount, 1974)
Producers: Irwin Winkler, Robert Chartoff
Director of Production: Hal Polaire
Assistant Directors: Ted Zachary, Tom Loforno
Screenplay: James Toback
Photography: Victor J. Kemper
Editing: Roger Spottiswoode
Set Decoration: Philip Rosenberg
Music: Jerry Fielding
Sound: Dennis Maitland
Cast: James Caan (Axel Freed), Paul Sorvino (Hips), Lauren Hutton (Billie),

Morris Carnovsky (A. R. Lowenthal), Jacqueline Brookes (Naomi), Burt Young (Carmine), Carmine Caridi (Jimmy), Carl W. Crudup (Spencer), Vic Tayback (One), Steven Keats (Howie), London Lee (Monkey), Antonio Fargas (pimp), Stuart Margolin (Cowboy), William Andrews, Joseph Attles, Ernest Butler, Sully Boyar, Gregory Rozakis, Starletta De Paur, Lucille Patton, Mitch Stein, J. Koshner, Charles Polk, M. E. Walsh, James Woods, Joel Wolfe
Running Time: 111 minutes
16mm Rental: Paramount Pictures

WHO'LL STOP THE RAIN (in Great Britain: **DOG SOLDIERS**) (United Artists, 1978)
Producers: Herb Jaffe, Gabriel Katzka
Associate Producers: Roger Spottiswoode, Sheldon Schrager
Coordination of Production: Marie-Carmen Jaffe
Directors of Production: Sheldon Schrager and (in Mexico) Alberto Ferrer
Assistant Directors: Arne Schmidt, Jerry Sobul, and (in Mexico) Jesus Marin
Screenplay: Judith Rascoe, Robert Stone
Photography: Richard H. Kline
Additional Photography: Ron Taylor
Editing: John Bloom, Chris Ridsdale, Mark Conte, and (in Mexico), Carlos Puente Portillo
Set Decoration: Dale Hennesy and (in Mexico) Augustin Ytuarte. Also Dianne Wager, Robert DeVestel, Enrique Estevez.
Special Effects: Paul Stewart, Jerry Williams, Kenneth Pepiot, Chuck Dolan
Music: Laurence Rosenthal
Sound Editing: Don Sharpe
Sound: Chris Newman and (in Mexico) José B. Carles.
Cast: Nick Nolte (Ray Hicks), Tuesday Weld (Marge Converse), Michael Moriarty (John Converse), Anthony Zerbe (Antheil), Richard Masur (Danskin), Ray Sharkey (Smitty), Gail Strickland (Charmian), Charles Haid (Eddie Peace), David Opatoshu (Bender), James Cranna (Gerald), Timothy Blake (Jody), Joaquin Martinez (Angel), Shelby Balik, Jean Howell, Jose Carlos Ruiz, John Durren, Bobby Kosser, Wings Hauser, Jonathan Banks, Michael Bair, Derrel Maury, Jan Burrell, Stuart Wilson, James Gavin, Bill Cross
Running Time: 126 minutes

Appendix: Showings of Reisz's Films at International Festivals

We Are the Lambeth Boys: Venice, Cork, Tours—all in 1959 (Prizes: Certificate of Merit at Cork, Grand Prix at Tours).

Momma Don't Allow: Montreal, 1966.

Saturday Night and Sunday Morning: Mar Del Plata, Moscow, Arnhem, Locarno, Venice—all in 1961 (Prizes: Best Picture at Mar Del Plata).

Night Must Fall: Berlin, 1964.

Morgan!: Cannes, Locarno, Montreal—all in 1966 (Prizes: at Cannes, Best Actress, Vanessa Redgrave).

Who'll Stop the Rain (Dog Soldiers): Cannes, 1978.

Index

165